Women Living with Broken Men

A Christian Perspective

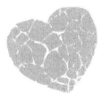

By Josephine Marie Ayers

Dedication

This book is dedicated to all the hurting men and women that for whatever reason, have suffered loss, abuse, dysfunction, abandonment and the like, in their lives.

I also dedicate this to my husband, David, who has taught me tenacity, and how to love in ways I could never imagine. He has also taught me that the circumstances we see, have depth and cause, far beyond the obvious.

Some names and identifying details have been changed to protect the privacy of individuals.

Any information in this book is not intended as a substitute for the medical advice of physicians. The reader should regularly consult a physician in matters relating to his/her health and particularly with respect to any symptoms that may require diagnosis or medical attention.

Published by Josephine Marie Ayers, Flames of Fire Ministries, Macedon, NY. All rights reserved.

Editing, Layout & Interior Design by Cheryl Jenkins, *Kingdom One Business Solutions*
Cover Design by Cheryl Jenkins, *Kingdom One Business Solutions*

ISBN-13: 978-1719024631
ISBN-10: 1719024634

Published in the United States of America

Acknowledgements

I want to thank Pastor Eric Scott, and Pastor Joshua Finley for walking this last part of my journey with me, as pastors, and as brothers in Christ. They gave me Godly counsel, support and were there for me at a very tough and crucial time. I am so thankful to God for them.

And last, but not least, to my Abba Daddy, who carried me, and still carries me even now. He was there even when I did not know Him. He held my heart, oh so tenderly then, and now.

I KNOW THAT HE KNOWS MY NAME!

Thank you, Jesus!

Endorsements

"It's the hope of the Gospel that transcends these transparent testimonies of women living with broken men. Josephine presents it clearly: our hope is in the promise of restoration so lavishly provided through the transforming power of Jesus Christ."

> ~Rev. Marjorie Stevens
> *Embracing Grace Ministries*

"There is Power in a testimony! Josephine shares her heart and past with a very open and honest transparency to offer an eternal hope and reconciliation for the future that is only found in the Savior - Jesus Christ.

After reading this book, these are the words that came to me: Broken vessels can still be filled with God's glory with the light of His Love shining through the cracks, and with several glazings of His faith to hold it all together!

The end result being far different than what we had in mind, but being at peace with what God has created.

Blessings to you Josephine and David. May you continue to grow in faith and love and fall deeper into His heart.

~David Lebo
Tidal Wave Ministries Int. Inc.
Author of *Abiding Under the Shadow*

"Jo Ayer's book, 'Women Living with Broken Men – A Christian Perspective,' is a book from the frontlines of brokenness to the glories of God's redemptive power. In raw fashion, Jo leads the reader through her broken marriage, but more importantly into the power of forgiveness and forgiveness' ability to bring about redemption.

Our lead pastor, Joshua Finley, and I walked with Jo through one phase of her walk with David, her precious husband, while we both served at Elim Gospel Church. There were many tears, reconciliations pursued by Jo, and always the prophetic voice of God leading the way to His redemptive purposes.

You will wonder how God could take such tangled messes and bring them around to His good. Yet, as Jo notes, there is a secret place of intimacy with Jesus that can untangle any mess – if we will only allow Him to lead the dance.

I pray you grow in hope as you see how God moved in Jo and David's lives, but even more, I pray you encounter the One who redeems us from the deepest pits - pits we often dig for ourselves, but He delights in leading us out of them."

~Eric Scott
Director of *Care and Connections Worship Center*
Lancaster, PA

$\mathcal{T}able\ of\ \mathcal{C}ontents$

Foreword

For years the family unit has been needing an upgrade. Broken homes, shattered dreams, divorces, dysfunctional family unit - all part of what needs to be fixed. We know that the only hope in today's world is the creator of the universe, Father God. The very name of this book, *Women Living with Broken Men* indicates the need for some knowledge in this area. You are holding on to one those helps for today's society. In this book, Josephine describes not only her journey as a woman who was affected by a broken man, but how she overcame the insecurities, heartache, and loneliness. The one and only hope for her was seeking the Lord and fully depending on him in all things.

Society today needs a good dose of hope! The journey that Josephine walked through, the hardest times of her life, and the progress she made when God fully took over in her heart demonstrates to all of just that... there is hope. Hope for healing, for restoration, and for hope to move forward with an attitude of joy. It seems that through our failures in life, we all tend to either become secluded, and push back any and all relationships in our lives, or we can be open, vulnerable and candidly honest with ourselves and others. If we chose the latter, it becomes a springboard for us to help others along in their life journey, no matter where it takes them.

When reading this book, I get the feeling that Josephine understands the importance of revealing her heart to others, assisting them in pursuing healing and getting them on the road to full recovery. This kind of action can only happen as one sees the importance of how their walk in life can lead others into full victory and acceptance of themselves - letting God use any situation for your good and His glory!

My wife and I see the need for families to be restored and healed. As the case with many, we pray that God will use others to bring that sense of awakening, bringing a renewed desire to be strong, powerful and make a difference. I believe that this book will take you into some delicate areas of your heart. There you will see where healing needs to take place, where strength needs to be renewed and where change needs to take place. The scriptures will come alive in your heart.

Knowing Josephine and Dave for over two decades, and personally see them walk through this journey has been quite amazing. As you read Dave's portion, you will be touched and awakened in your own heart as to how the Lord can change a broken man and make him into a man of encouragement and strength. His view and perspective will brighten your day and give men the desire to see a change in their own heart. Be encouraged. God can take any situation and make it a good one! Why? Because He is a good God; One that cares about each and every one of us in our personal walk. As you read this book, keep your heart open and attentive. See where the Lord wants to restore in you. See how He wants to bring you into the place of full and complete confidence in Him. This book will help you get to that point. It will bring you to a place of full understanding that God cares about you and is right there for you in any given situation.

Mark A. Griffo
Stronger Together Ministries
www.MarkandDeborah.org

Introduction

Why this topic of women living with broken men? One, because broken people make more broken people, and two, because I myself, have had several unfortunate experiences in this area. I know that I am not the only one.

This subject I have written about is limited in scope and detail due to the enormity and delicacy of the subject. The principles and/or solutions that I am sharing are not all inclusive, but limited to what I felt led by the Holy Spirit to share at this time.

Being successfully married is a challenging journey in itself. However, if one or both partners are broken, it becomes even more challenging. When you have broken couples, you have broken children, and so on and so forth. Are there answers? Yes, indeed!

There are many different types of broken relationships. Children with either parent, siblings, friendships and marital. God is all about relationship, so is it any wonder that the attack on relationships is and has been probably the number one strategy of the enemy, since the beginning of time? However, God is also about reconciliation, healing, and restoration.

I believe one of the main reasons that our world is in

such distress is the erosion of the family unit. Since the Garden of Eden, Satan's strategy has been to destroy the family unit, and then destroy the world. He is the real enemy here. Although this book is geared towards women, men have similar struggles as well, I am sure. The last chapter is an admonition to men, from a broken man.

When I was involved in women's prison ministry, I can tell you that EVERY woman had a story about having had a majorly dysfunctional family. There was one group of women that stood out from the others... those of Hebrew descent. I had heard a comment from the prison leadership, that basically declared that in the prison system there were very few Hebrew inmates, compared to other nationalities. Why? Because the family unit is very strong in this culture. That is a confirming statement, arguing the point for healthy, morally, and spiritually sound family units that acknowledge Jesus! Why?

As I stated, I have had several experiences of this nature and only now, many years later, do I have an understanding as to why those relationships failed, at least to some degree. I can also appreciate why most broken relationships fail, and why mine did not survive. I also understand how being a follower of Jesus Christ helped me to survive and come to terms with some of the issues in my situations. Sometimes, resolutions do not come the way we think they should. However, there seems to be a definite 'Plan B' available to us.

I know of many women who have walked this road, and I aspire to offer hope to them. I also hope to share a Christian man's perspective in how he worked his way through this difficult experience. One other thing I want to point out is that the enemy of our souls loves to isolate us: to make us think we are all alone in our pain. But in reality, that is far from the truth!

I know from my experiences that GOD will work all things together for good, even when we make some wrong choices. The secret is, I believe, when our hearts are postured in radical obedience, dependence, and submission to Him, and we are seeking to do His will. When we diligently seek after Him and we miss it, be assured He WILL turn it around for good. It's a covenant promise. All of us on this earth are called to His purposes. Whether we seek Him and His purpose out or not, is our choice. But it is His heart.

Romans 8:26-28 says, *"Meanwhile, the moment we get tired in the waiting, God's Spirit is right alongside helping us along. If we don't know how or what to pray, it doesn't matter. He does our praying in and for us, making prayer out of our wordless sighs, our aching groans. He knows us far better than we know ourselves, knows our present condition, and keeps us present before God. That's why we can be so sure that every detail in our lives of love for God is worked into something good."* (The Message Bible - MSG)

This is an ever-present reality for me. I have found that my mistakes and even things that go wrong almost always turn out better. So, my perspective in all of this is, that when it goes awry, I look for and expect the better thing that will happen because His word says that! He is building a strong track record with me for this.

In addition, having Jesus in my life has been the reason I am not just standing today, but thriving. My heart is for ALL women; hurting women. I believe my journey has had a purpose. My heart is also for the men that, not by choice I'm sure, have been walking in dysfunction. I hope to share some stories, not just from myself, but from others who have passed this way, and offer hope for the future for others.

I would not have been able to write this book without going through the difficult times. Looking back, I can see that God used my trials as a blessing. That was the lesson for me and for you; when I was in my darkest valley, His strong Hand was leading me.

Offering Hope,
Rev. Josephine Marie Ayers

Perspective

For the purpose of this book, I want to define what perspective is. According to *Webster's Online Dictionary*, perspective is defined as *"a particular attitude toward, or way of regarding something; a point of view."*

For example, take a partial glass of water. How we see it says a lot about our perspective on things. Do we see it as half-full or half-empty?

In the following pages, we will look at things from three perspectives: the female's view, God's view, and the view from a 'broken' man. Broken meaning, according to *Webster's Dictionary*, *"having been fractured or damaged, and no longer in one piece or in working order."*

As we look into Scripture, we can see the propensity toward brokenness in men, women and families started in the Garden of Eden, with Adam and Eve. I believe that the enemy of our souls knew from the beginning the power of the family unit. You can see how the devil played on Eve's weakness as a human, and deceived her. Her man, Adam, could have stopped it right there, but in his humanness, put the seal on our need for a Savior. Sin came into the world, and it was all downhill after that.

Dysfunction entered our world. Look at their offspring, Cain and Abel; jealousy and murder were next on the list. If you notice, it started with Adam and Eve's deception, and consequent disobedience. Jesus bore the curse of all of these sins on the cross, but the propensity toward learned behaviors still exists. In other words, we still tend to do those things we see, rather than what we know is truth. We come into this world a blank slate, and whomever is in our sphere of influence, writes all over us. We become what we see, hear, and are taught.

From all appearances in our world today, we can see the forces of good and evil are consistently colliding. Fortunately, for us as believers, we know that eventually the Cross gets the last word in every situation. God does not leave us without a blueprint for getting through our trials. He is looking for overcomers. So, although He is there to help us, he does allow hard things to cross our paths, to test us.

The Bible talks about this in the book of Job. The Bible also tells us we will have trials, but good things will come out of them, if we allow them to work for us. **The Bible is our blueprint!**

Romans 5:3-5 says: *"And not only this, but we also exult in our tribulations, knowing that tribulation brings about perseverance; and perseverance, proven character; and proven character, hope; and hope does not disappoint, because the love of God has been poured out within our hearts through the Holy Spirit who was given to us."* (NASB)

I can really identify with this!!! I'd like to think I will become a "tempered steel of virtue". I'm not there yet, for sure.

Some people's perspectives are bleak. It's hard to overcome when you cannot see the light for the journey from Point A to Point C; when you cannot even fathom what 'B' looks like. To some, there is no 'B'. That is where the enemy wants to keep us... hopeless, and feeling alone. Truth is, there IS a PLAN B; it is His way!

Please bear in mind we are not 'doomed' to be whatever we have been programmed to be our entire lives. That is also a lie from the "pit of Hell". We do have choices along the way. Even when we have learned the "wrong" thing, it can be undone or relearned.

Jesus offers hope and redemption. Christianity is all about change. I don't know about you, but change for me was "scary". Unfortunately, many women in tough situations would rather accept the abuse, than accept the changes that could bring about good and freedom. That being said, they stay in difficult circumstances and continue to subject themselves and maybe even their children, to more pain and abuse. There is a risk for the children to learn those bad behaviors and continue the abuse cycle. One of the issues that impedes change is fear; fear of the retribution they may incur if they try to break the cycle they are in. Please note: when God is in the changes we need to make, He paves the way. It is so important to tune into His will, and stay close to Him. Change is never easy, but necessary, and doable, if He is in the equation. Been there and done that! I believe when we stop the process of change in our lives we become "stagnant"and then figuratively "dead".

Fear of failure is another obstacle to change. Women in abusive situations suffer from low self-esteem. Many are told they can never succeed at anything - another lie from the pit! I, myself, have experienced this. The Lord showed me that failure is a normal part of the 'learning curve'. Instead of letting this type of fear stop us, we need to embrace mistakes and learn from them, instead of dreading making them. Failure can be a strong motivator to growth and change. Joseph, in the Bible, learned from his mistakes and learned the art of 'holding his counsel'. Please see Bible reference under appendices and read the story for yourself.

One of my favourite scriptures that helped me press through was Psalm 107. Throughout that passage, most of the verses end with, *"Then they cried unto the Lord in their trouble, and He saved them out of their distresses."* (KJV)

It starts with the willingness to embrace the issues, motivation to change, and hope that life can be different, no matter what has happened in your life. It is called faith and hope.

The Bible defines faith in Hebrews 11:11, *"Now faith is the substance of things hoped for, the evidence of things not seen."* (KJV)

Frequently, in the midst of our personal whirlwind, it is easy to lose faith, and hope (excited expectation), and get caught up in the situation and begin to sink. We can have a 'bleak' perspective... BUT GOD! In fact, there are many portions of scripture that actually say He is in the whirlwind. God spoke to Job out of the whirlwind when he was going through the dark night of his soul.

I can remember a few years back. I took several wrong exits during a horrible storm, because I could not see. I ended up driving right into a tornado. I could not see one thing, except the white lines on the right side of the road. I was listening in my spirit as I was trying to manage the incredibly bad weather, road conditions, and a car that was sounding like it would stall at any moment. What I heard in my spirit was, "Keep your eyes on the white line. Follow the white line." God was in my literal whirlwind, as I believe the Holy Spirit was the spiritual white line I was following.

I could feel the tentacles of fear attempting to grip me while driving and I had to fight them off. I had just come from a powerful reconciliation meeting. I finally reasoned to myself that God would not allow such a victory and then sink my ship on the expressway in this storm. While thinking this out, fear left, and the realization of the enemy's strategy to derail me, became an "ah-ha" moment. It took a long time, but I did get home safely.

The interesting thing about this situation was that every wrong exit I took, the weather became better and better. God had His hand on all my mistakes and was clearly my "co-pilot".

Remember, FEAR can keep us from moving forward, trying new things, changing old things and ultimately has the potential to immobilize us. There are actually more than 365 "Fear not..." verses in the Bible. So, you'd think we would get the memo!

Again, it seems like all the stories we hear on TV and through media are centered around the battle for good versus evil. These days, it is all around us. Fortunately, for the Christian, we know from the

Bible that again, the cross WILL get the last word. We know how the story ends; the Bible tells us so. God has given all of us a 'white line to follow'. The choice is up to us; will we follow it or not?

Another great story about walking by faith rather than fear is seen in the story of the three men in the fire; Shadrach, Meshach and Abednego. They were tossed into a fiery furnace. What was visible, was a 4th man with them. GOD, Himself kept them safe and they came out unscathed.

Please read Daniel, Chapter 3:16-25: *"Shadrach, Meshach, and Abednego answered King Nebuchadnezzar, "Your threat means nothing to us. If you throw us in the fire, the God we serve can rescue us from your roaring furnace and anything else you might cook up, O king. But even if he doesn't, it wouldn't make a bit of difference, O King. We still wouldn't serve your gods or worship the gold statue you set up."*

Nebuchadnezzar, his face purple with anger, cut off Shadrach, Meshach, and Abednego. He ordered the furnace fired up seven times hotter than usual. He ordered some strong men from the army to tie them up, hands and feet, and throw them into the roaring furnace. Shadrach, Meshach, and Abednego, bound hand and foot, fully dressed from head to toe, were pitched into the roaring fire. Because the king was in such a hurry and the furnace was so hot, flames from the furnace killed the men who carried Shadrach, Meshach, and Abednego to it, while the fire raged around Shadrach, Meshach, and Abednego.

Suddenly King Nebuchadnezzar jumped up in alarm and said, "Didn't we throw three men, bound hand and foot, into the fire?"

"That's right, O king," they said.

"But look!" he said. "I see four men, walking around freely in the fire, completely unharmed! And the fourth man looks like a son of the gods!" (MSG)

Indeed, it was Jesus Himself walking amongst them, and they walked out of that furnace more than alive!

Is your perspective changing? Maybe from bleak to hopeful, that God has not forgotten your address; that if we were able to see in the spirit we would see those heavenly forces with us, protecting us? Just when you think you are alone, you are NOT!

That fear is from the devil, and even though you cannot see GOD, He is still with you. I cannot stress that enough. Again, one of the enemy's strategies is isolation. He wants you to think you are alone!

In 2 Kings 6:16-17, *"Elisha said, 'Don't be afraid, for those who are with us outnumber those who are with them.' Then Elisha prayed, 'Lord, please open his eyes and let him see.' So, the Lord opened the servant's eyes. He looked and saw the mountain was covered with horses and chariots of fire all around Elisha."* (HCSB)

I know some folks say God would never do miracles for them. It is called unworthiness. The devil tries to cover you with shame and unworthiness. You cannot buy into that! It is a lie. I also had to clearly believe that any condemnation coming against me is not from God.

Romans 8:1 *"Therefore, there is now no condemnation for those who are in Christ Jesus."* (NIV)

Again, this is another strategy from the devil. Not because I say so, because the Bible tells me so. The Bible says He is no respecter of persons. He is a Father, first and foremost, and loves ALL of His children and would have that none would perish.

John 3:16 (NIV) *"For God so loved the world that he gave his one and only Son, that whoever believes in him shall not perish but have eternal life."*

How do you know a lie? Well you have to educate yourself with the truth! Where do you find the truth? It is found in His Living Word, the Bible! If the enemy, the devil, can cut you off from reading God's Word, then all these things will be like concrete shoes on our feet, and static on our spiritual lines.

Freedom in Christ

Galatians 5:1 *"It is for freedom that Christ has set us free. Stand firm, then, and do not let yourselves be burdened again by a yoke of slavery."* (NIV)

We do not know why we go through trials, or why deliverance is not fast. We can only say He will be with us and will deliver us. Oh, God, help us in our unbelief!!!

He does take care of His own.

Isaiah 43:1-2 *"But now, this is what the Lord says - he who created you, Jacob, he who formed you, Israel: "Do not fear, for I have redeemed you; I have summoned you by name; you are mine. When you pass through the waters, I will be with you; and when you pass through the rivers, they will not sweep over you. When you walk through the fire, you will not be burned; the flames will not set you ablaze."* (NIV)

God sent His only begotten Son to this earth to remedy the situation, to bring us back into relationship with GOD the Father, to heal and restore our identity in Him and mend a whole lot of cracked pots. Jesus is here to change our perspective. I can attest to the fact that it works!

In Psalm 91, God says that *"He that dwells in the secret place shall abide under the shadow of the Almighty."* I asked the Lord once, "What is the Secret Place?" A closet? Nope. What He impressed on me was that the "secret place" was the intimate knowledge of His love; and that once we connected with that love, we would realize that nothing can harm us, and that we are not at the mercy of the enemy, but at the mercy of God Almighty.

That revelation diffused many fears in my life. I think far too often, when living in tough situations with people that demean and undermine us, it is difficult to believe we are loved by man, or God. This is another lie of the enemy. God loved us so much He sent His only begotten son to save us from hell and reconcile us to His Father. He will never stop pursuing us. It is actually us that runs from Him.

I remember having a difficult time understanding or feeling that love. Then God showed me every time I was shown a blessing or received a hug from someone that had the fullness of Christ, it was actually Him loving me, through them. That's when I had that moment of finally connecting the fact that God had been loving me all along, throughout my life. I began to experience His love in a more profound and intimate way. I also perceived that as I ministered to others, it is His love I share in the same manner, to others. Did you know that God loves us, just because we ARE; because we are fearfully and WONDERFULLY made? That's the truth! See Psalm 139.

I also began to see that there is actually more working *for* me, than against me. Again, it's about perspective.

Focusing on how many times I had been loved as opposed to focusing on those around me who had beat me down, physically or emotionally. It helped me to know He is always with me. I am tucked in that secret place of the intimate knowledge of HIS love, and so can you be. When you are tucked in that secret place, you almost feel 'bulletproof'. God is always jealous and protective over us. He is singing over us! Zephaniah 3:17. There is a new-found confidence that we get in that place. Truly no weapon formed against us can prosper. (Isaiah 54:17 - Authors paraphrase) When we get to this place, fear has NO grip! It's up to us not to let it in, again. We need to take all those thoughts captive! 2 Corinthians 10:14

We talked about all things working together for good (Romans 8:28). I am at a place now tha when things do not work out, instead of getting upset I look to see how God is going to rewrite my story for the better. He has never disappointed me!

My Story

What can I say? I was an only child, and my family focus was that I would have a good education. Relationships were difficult; I lived pretty much around adults, in a rural environment.

I also grew up with comments like, *"You are a good for nothing! You will never to amount to anything."* This was something I had to unlearn at a later time. As an adult I would see that it was an attempt, by certain adults in my sphere of influence, to shame me into excellence. I had a good family life, and then at age 12 the bottom fell out. My dad left us, for another woman. My mom was very overprotective and I again found out later on why, but what did I know at the time? I took my dad's leaving very hard. My mom struggled to support herself and me. She was also taking care of her ill mother at the same time. I excelled in academia, to prove I was good for, and at, something. But I felt very controlled. I also felt that unless I was perfect, I would not be accepted. To make matters worse I was bullied and rejected in school. This set the pattern for the many mistakes and wrong choices I would make, and follow later on in life.

As a teen, I had this need to crawl out from under my family of origin's control. As I said, I created an avalanche of mistakes. I found myself trying find a 'man' to replace the love of my father. I had lost my natural father at a pivotal age, and I began looking for love in all the wrong places. But one thing I will say about my family of origin: there was never yelling, screaming, rage or anger. I was introduced to that when I married! For all practical purposes, I thought I had a happy family. My parents, if they had discord never showed that in front of me. Hence when dad left, I hit the ground and hard!

I got pregnant and was married at 19. Now, I was a teenager having a child. What did I know? I was running from parental control into the arms of someone who exerted more control over me than my parents did. Not only that, I did not have confidence, good self-esteem or survival skills, so when the roof fell in, I felt trapped.

I became an RN (Registered Nurse) and excelled in that. That occupation became my new identity. But when that ended, years later, I lost "me" again. My identity was rooted in what I *did*, not who I *was*. I was a daughter of the Most-High God, and also a 'son' of GOD, with all the same rights of inheritance.

Did I know Jesus back then as a resource? No. I loved God, but had no knowledge of the bible, or any biblical principles. I had religion back then and was never taught I could have relationship with Jesus. My focus was not on Jesus, or the Holy Spirit.

The person I married was as young as me, and I found out much later, and too late, that he was an abused child. He made me feel less than adequate. Although I was 'saved' during that marriage, I had no one to disciple me. So, in essence, I was doing this new-found Christianity my way. I had minimal understanding of what I was reading in the Bible. I also had very low self-esteem.

I had read a book called *"How to be the Wife of a Happy Husband"* by Darien B. Cooper. I followed its principles, which were Christian, to the 'T'. I knew I was different. I saw and felt changes in my life. When my husband did not respond, the abuse to me and the children worsened. I asked him to leave. The stronger I got, the worse he got. I got mixed up with another man and then repented. I admitted my error and we got back together. But things got worse, not better.

I ended up in the hospital at one point, and our doctor called my mate into accountability. The doctor told him she knew of the abuse, and if he did not get into therapy, she would report him to CPS. He did go for counselling when confronted, but nothing changed. It got worse. He did not get counselling because he felt he needed help, he did it to avoid a child protective charge. You need to want to be helped, and realize you need it, to get help.

I felt alone in that hospital room, but some amazing things began to happen. One of those instances was when another patient wandered into my room, and gave me a message. She said that Jesus sent her there to encourage me, and that I was not alone.

Another time a pastor visited me gave me Psalm 91. It is an amazing psalm of protection. As I said, I knew little of the Bible, but looking back I can see how even in my dark night of the soul, I was getting messages from heaven. God was in control; He had this! I have so many of these encouragements that God sent to me! I see more now, looking back, than I did then.

When we finally broke up, my heart was to protect my two children, even though at that point it was too late. It had nothing to do with me not loving their father; that made it even harder to separate from him. They had already been scarred in their young lives. Now, I had two very broken children on my hands. What a mess I had created! I struggled for almost three years, but I ended up losing my children anyway. Their dysfunction was too great. What was explained to me, by the counselors, was that my children had learned how to abuse mom, from their dad. They thought that women needed to be controlled. So, when the man of the house was gone, they took that role over. Because of the situation I chose divorce. Remember, broken people make more broken people, unless the cycle is somehow interrupted. I had waited too long to change things.

I believe my youth and rebellion got me into this pickle! I was running from my parent's control and ended up in a worse situation. Because of some unfair rules, even though I had full custody, I ended up separated from my younger child for 7 years, my older for 3 years. Much later on, God restored the relationships between myself and both of my children. There is a price to pay for bad decisions.

My children went through a whole lot, but they took their issues and turned them into success stories. Both knew Jesus! In fact, looking back the older boy said if he had not been through the trials he endured, he would not be the man he is today! So, in spite of the mistakes I made, God made some good come out of this mess. I now have 5 grandchildren. It was a very long, hard road though. I am leaving out a lot of details as this story could be a book in itself.

Fast forward to now. God chased down my ex-husband, and he is now a mighty man of God, but not withstanding what he had to go through to get there. We are now friends in fact. After a period of time, I came back to New York. The Lord prompted me to contact him with a birthday card. He responded almost immediately. God had also been working on him. Later that year, he asked me to water baptize him. I did! I think the power there was in my forgiving him, and him forgiving me. God will chase us down; He loves us so. His Word says He would have that none would perish. We need to have a global view that this world is not the be all and end all. There is a Heaven and a very hot Hell! The thing I found about him was that he was very ill and infirmed. He himself attributed that to the unforgiveness and bitterness he had toward me for 35 years. More truth! Now please note things like this don't often happen, but it did for me. Reconciliation still needs to happen between him and our sons. But he did his part in owning his part in our family mess.

Two and a half years after that journey was over, I was lonely. I made a bigger mistake! I did have a 'check in my spirit', but my need for a man and feeling affirmed by a man, led me into an almost deadly relationship. After five years of hell, and nine separations, it ended. I literally went from the proverbial 'frying pan into the fire'. This person used Christianity as a tool of manipulation; to hook me. He had what I would call an evil discerning spirit. All the boxes on my list that needed to be "checked" for another relationship were addressed, without him even knowing. Again, I did not ask God. I was still on the "throne" of my life. But God was in that whirlwind as well.

Not only that, but for a brief period, I allowed this man to deceive me into putting recreation and intimacy first, and God last. I remember vividly when I took a stand for God. All hell literally broke loose! Years of physical, sexual, and emotional abuse ensued. He even wanted to kill me. I was under some kind of "spell" with this man, and when I finally cried out to the Lord for deliverance, He answered! Again another longer story there's not room for in this book!

Just after the final separation, I found out that this man, my husband, was sleeping with another woman that I knew; in my house and in my bed! I had suspected infidelity, but had no solid proof. This man had been injured before he left me, from a boating accident. Previous to that, I prayed deliverance like never before. God answered and took it all out of my hands.

When his mistress came to my house, she kept mumbling something about being sorry. Hmm, sorry for what, I thought. Then she said it, "I have been sleeping with your husband, in your house, in your bed for 2 and a half years." What???!! I promptly asked her to leave and I cannot even tell you the emotions that went through me. Rage, anger and betrayal were amongst the many. I began throwing frozen food on the floor. I just could not believe my ears!

I called my doctor and asked for an appointment. I felt violated, betrayed and scared. But God protected me! I knew I wanted more detail. Well, this "other woman" called me back and asked if we could talk. I agreed. She came over, and as we were talking she kept asking for my forgiveness. The Holy Spirit was prodding me. But somehow, I did not believe her. Then I thought since my husband was a violent man, and she knew it, I challenged her to call him and tell him that she had confessed all to me. She agreed! I knew where he was and dialed the number. He answered. I heard both of their conversations, as they were quite loud. I finally heard her say, "I don't know; it must be God!" Surely, I thought, what does this woman know about GOD?

When she was done I asked her about what she knew about God. The whole time she was talking, the Holy Spirit kept prodding me. She kept asking for my forgiveness. Then she said, "my heart feels so dirty". Then out it came from my mouth, "I know someone who can help you feel clean!" I had her attention. She said, "Who?" I gave her the Gospel message and then and there she asked God for forgiveness. I forgave her, and she became a child of God. In fact, we told her husband together the next night, and he forgave her.

Please note: my decision to forgive her was literally an act of obedience to GOD, with no feeling behind it. Those feelings would and did come later.

Years later I got a letter from her, saying that their marriage of over 24 years was more solid than ever. What would have happened if I had not been obedient and forgiven her? I shudder to think. That was one of the hardest things I have done in my life. A few years later I lead my ex-husband's daughter to Jesus. I had to forgive him, for me! I forgave him, but I did not have to live with him anymore. She also did admit to me that he had plotted to kill me.

When I look back on this, I can see that sometimes God uses us in situations that we would not sign up for voluntarily. All of us have choices. Bad choices equal bad consequences. Good choices equal good consequences. I feel that two souls entered the kingdom in the whirlwind of my mess. My expectations for marriage had failed me for the second time; another fairytale had exploded. But God did make some good come out of it! He also protected me from dangers that I had no knowledge about.

The one thing that was a common denominator in my 1st and 2nd marriages was that I never asked God what

His will was for either of these relationships.

Point #1: Seek the Lord in ALL things.

Fresh Start

At this point in my life (1992) I got down on my knees and threw up the white flag. I recommitted my life to Jesus, and as I prayed, "Lord, I have failed over and over and over. It is time to do it your way, ALL your way. You can tell me what to wear, what to eat, and what to do, I am wholly Yours! Do with me what You will."

I purposed in my heart to follow Him anywhere, and that He would be my Husband, the greatest husband I could ever have.

I went to a different church, and I remember the pastor there started praying for me for a godly husband. I said, "Please don't; I am done." I gave him the time out sign. I have never done that before in a prayer.

That year I began an amazing journey with Jesus. It was then He introduced me to my prophetic gifting. I had it all along, but in those years, it was named ESP.

I had no idea it was from God. It was quite amazing. I had a whole year of rest, and the most amazing supernatural experiences with God.

I began to get a steady flow of prophetic words in which I was the recipient. It was all so amazing. I felt literally, as if God had hit the reset button in my life. These words were a demonstration of God's love for me in "real time." I began to see Him go out of His way to tell me, through His people, that I did have purpose and a plan in the Kingdom. Hope was restored to me. By the way, this is one of the purposes of prophecy; to encourage and exhort. I began to know my God in a more intimate way than I had ever known Him before.

I had done what God had been waiting for me to do my entire life; sell out to Him with radical obedience. It was Jesus and I, and I was so happy. I had a new identity revealed to me, that of a daughter of the King. I knew intellectually of His love, but this year I felt it. Every time a believer hugged me, it was Him in a human suit. God did know me, love me, deliver me and give me hope and a future.

Each day was a new great adventure. I could hear His voice so clearly. It was not audible, but a sensing of His voice. In fact, it sounded a whole lot like me, but with words that I would not normally come up with.

He began training me to act on His voice, and He

always confirmed it later on. He was providing for me in ways I could have never thought of. I had my hope and joy back, and it did not depend on another man. I always knew of God's love in my head, but I was now, firsthand, letting the Master pamper me. Now He was leading me in all of my life. Not only that, but I was getting some serious healing in my life from all the trauma and hurt. I was avidly pursing my Bridegroom and He was daily meeting me.

I started going to a woman's prayer group. I also started a nursing home ministry and had many friends. I was part of a large prayer chain, as well.

Somewhere in the course of that year, an elder came to me and said that God could not give me all that He had for me unless I opened my hand. I knew what that meant. I was not open to getting married or seeing men again. No way!!!

God had to heal my opinion, and my perspective of men. I had to forgive the male gender. I was not ready. I told my older son, "Two strikes and you're out!" He said, 'No, Mom, its three strikes and you're out!!"

While God was working behind the scenes, I took a scriptural counseling course based on Jay Adams' books. The focus in his counseling techniques boiled down to getting our relationship straight with GOD, not pointing out and complaining about the other person's issues. The biblical principles centered around the scripture that says, *"When a man pleases the Lord he makes even his enemies to be at peace with them."* *Proverbs 16:7* (HCSB)

While I was a member of that singles prayer chain, the male in charge of the chain kept calling my number with requests. He said he always talked to my answering machine. One night, he got me on a real voice call. He mentioned a cousin of his had tried to commit suicide and told me where she was. I felt led to go to the hospital. I met him there and ended up leading his cousin to Jesus. He said he was "impressed by my boldness." He asked me out for coffee. But as far as I was concerned, he was only a friend.

I used to go roller-skating with the singles once a week, and he would be there. This one week he came out to me on the rink and grabbed my hand, and we skated the whole night. I had blisters on my feet. I could not skate very well; it was more like "ice walking" or holding on to the rail around the rink! He said he felt sorry for me.

Long story short, God was bringing feelings into my heart, and we ended up being closer friends. I knew I was starting to care for him.

In the meantime, the Lord was challenging me in this new prophetic walk. He laid it on my heart to put my mobile home up for sale, and I would know where I was going by June of the next year. This was December. I knew His voice and found a Spirit-filled sister to list it.

The challenges from God were getting more and more audacious. But He came through on all of them. Special note: God was building a track record with Him of miracles. As the challenges in my life became larger and larger, I had this history to glean from, to know somehow, He would come through again. I could feel and sense His hand on my life.

I was planning a trip to California and Israel, back to back. I was going to visit my son in California, and then home and off to Israel. On the plane to California, I got a scripture and the Lord told me I would be telling my older son, then in the Navy, that I was getting married. Oh dear, to who? Is this you, God? But God had already started preparing me for my husband. I was at a point in my life where I wanted a man, which was different than needing a man. I finally had come to terms with my stand-alone identity in Him. It was the most exciting year of my life, with Him!

Point # 2: When contemplating a relationship, we need to have our identity in Him established.

In this case, two halves DO NOT make a whole.

If you think your identity and purpose are in another person, you are wrong. Hence, the difference in this last journey was; I did not NEED a man. I came to him willingly wanting to share my own life with him. I also wanted to see how we could blend our different selves and do life together. I wanted to serve God with this person.

Point # 3: God will define and establish us, not other humans.

While I was in California visiting my son, this man asked me to marry him. We got married in April, and my mobile home sold in June, all cash! It had happened exactly as God had said it would. We had an apartment set aside for us from God. That is a whole other story!

You can bet we both sought the Lord, and hard! I

knew that I knew that I knew that God was wanting me to marry this man. He felt the same as well. We had so many confirmations. We had kept it pure until our wedding day; it was so great and happy.

You Can't Get Orange Juice from a Grapefruit

One month after our wedding day, it all started to fall apart. In the midst of this, the Lord told me He was sending us to California for ministry. I thought, who will take care of mom? I was an only child, and all my support systems were here. By the way, the Lord answered me with, 'Excuse Me, who is your support system"? He had me there. I thought I would fix this by not telling David. That was May. The following November David came to me and told me that God had told him he was to quit his job and move us to California. So much for trying to outsmart God! Yikes!

I had a real feeling I could only describe as 'wither', when the abuse started. I knew that I knew I had heard God on this. I was now fearful of this impending move clear across the country, that I thought was God.

Now I was terrified this man I married seemed to be very naïve, gullible, and did not know most of what other people knew. What was this, Lord? He was an excellent electrician, mechanic, etc., but emotionally there were some major issues. So, here we are moving to California? Who's going to take care of me? He does not seem to have a clue about most things, most people know. No answer from the Throne Room.

Needleless to say, it all fell together, and we moved to California and lived there 14 years. Mom came out to be with us and passed on to heaven there. It was an incredible spiritual journey and fill up. Many miracles happened there; many divine connections. We loved it there for many reasons, and I even told God, please don't ever move me back East. Big mistake, He did much later on. He also did it in a way that I had no choice.

But the marriage was rocky, empty. He worked endless hours and I was alone a lot. I found out 23 years later that I had put some incredible expectations on him that he could never fill. He was solidly 'broken.' He was not 'wired' that way, I would find out many, many years later.

Point # 4: Expectations on other people are seldom realistic, keep your eyes on Jesus.

What are some definitions of the word "expectation"? My understanding of the word is that it can be a strong belief that something of the same nature will happen in the future; or an anticipation of something happening.

I remember when I had my first son. He was such an easy baby. He ate, slept, pooped, and was happy to play for hours by himself. No colic, not a lot of illness, nothing.

I thought, this mom thing is not so hard, after all. Then four and a half years later came his brother. I just assumed, based on my first experience, number two baby would be the same. What a shock I was in for! Not even close. In fact, everything was opposite with him. He was my high maintenance baby, child, and young adult. Was it his fault? No. In fact, knowing myself, and as young as I was back then, if I had him first there might not have been another child. God wanted him here on this planet as much as his brother. I almost feel that God, knowing me, gave me Chris first, so I would be willing to have more. I was not prepared for this shock.

Is it not the truth with us? We base our expectations on past experiences, or maybe even other's experiences. This is an instant recipe for disappointment, disillusionment, and failure. Most of the time it is not even the other person's fault. The actual phrase, "You cannot get orange juice from a grapefruit," came from my husband. He used to say this all the time to me. I thought he was being sarcastic and got angry back. The whole time he was trying to say, "I just cannot give you what you need, Jo. I am not wired that way." Ladies, we need to be discerning and listen to the cry of the other person's heart. I should have instituted the speaker-listener technique with him I learned in counseling, and say something like, "What I heard you say was....," and continue to do so back and forth, until we finally came to a mutual understanding. This is so valuable in communicating with people.

Isn't it also the way we form our opinions of our Heavenly Father's love for us? If we had a great earthly dad, love is not an issue. However, if we did not, we may transpose our negative experiences on God. Our perception of God may be so tainted that it can keep us from bringing many to Him. As unfortunate as that reality is, it is truth.

When in fact, our Heavenly Father's love does not

even come close to any human's love for us. It is like a multifaceted diamond, with endless light, glimmer and angles. So much height, depth, and width that our human mind cannot wrap itself around it.

We need to understand that the standard for love has to come from the Bible and the truth about God's love written there; not our limited experiences, definitions, or expectations of love.

So, based on our perceptions and expectations, others fail miserably as they do not measure up, and often never will.

I thought my marriage to David would be 'happily ever after' like the fairy tale. There are no fairy tales. Often the assignments we get are based on GOD's expectations of us, because He knows what we can do in Him. Even now, after 25 years, I am just beginning to unpack what my journey with him is all about.

If it had not been for me keeping my eyes on Jesus, His sustaining grace, and His plans, purposes and will for my life, I probably would have failed in this assignment. I would have missed this blessing and the sharing of this testimony before God and others. My focus was on the prize of His overcoming power in this situation. He is looking for overcomers. I could not veer off the original direction. The secret I knew was that it was God that brought us together. My expectation was that finally someone was going to take care of me. Well, the truth is, God was and is the one taking care of both of us, then and now. My eyes are fixed on Him, as is He is my husband.

Point #5: When all else fails, and things look bleak, stand on the original direction and word you got from the Lord, and do not waiver.

In spite of it all, God never gave me release from this relationship, or him. Actually, I never asked him to be released. This was it and we were bound and determined to make sense of it. He tried to escape our marriage many times, but fear gripped him and I found out later, he was so broken that the challenges we had in California were way over his head. Even though God always came through for us, this world he was in was very frightening. I was trying to get orange juice from a grapefruit. It was not going to happen. He will admit he was doing the same with me. I made an attitude adjustment. When we look to each other to fulfill all of our needs; that is another recipe for disappointment and failure.

Point #6: You will never get orange juice from a grapefruit.

His family added more stress to our relationship. They blamed me for taking him from the family. It was never so, but quite the opposite. It was actually David that heard the call to leave his family. They apparently knew he was 'different' and felt threatened by me, especially when we moved to California. We were no longer under their watchful eye. They did not trust me or believe me.

Also, during that time, my mate began to present with some **serious** issues. I knew something was very wrong. I did not know what, and even though I knew Jesus better than ever, I thought I missed some very important markers. But there were too many incredible things that happened along the way that reinforced our marriage. In spite of all I knew, he was my intended. If I had it to do again, I would make the same decision. I know that God told me he was the one! The Lord had indicated the same to David. I will admit I was confused, but I had to trust God with this. If I had known all I do now, I would have run. But God knew that about me as well.

Things went from bad to worse very quickly. My love did not seem to know things that most adults know. He was extremely gifted in trade skills, yet he could not seem to apply the analytical skills he had in electronics, mechanics etc., to real life.

In lieu of my past failures, I began to think there was something wrong with me. I would have amazing conversations with God, something like, "Lord, you know all the pain of my past, so why are You allowing this to happen again?" I felt like a real loser, and perhaps my lot in life was just to suffer.

But the one thing I can say now that I could not say before, was that I had NOT made a mistake, and I knew God was in this pain, the whirlwind and all! In 2007 after mom passed, many very hard things happened. I had a terrible meltdown. I was useless. David did not step up to the plate to care for me, or work. He was scared and grieving as well. I still did not get that something was seriously wrong with him that prevented him from making good decisions while I was out of commission. We ended up losing an entire storage unit, and two paid off vehicles. We were actually homeless for three months as well. I finally gave in to coming back to NY. It was clear God was closing the door on California. While He used my mate to drag me out there, He also used him to drag me back East. We came back to New York in 2008 (In fact, it was 08/08/08) with 5 cardboard boxes, two suitcases, and a laptop! Who knew? While we were in California, we had the most incredible spiritual education and experiences. I did do full time ministry. Little did I know that was 'school' for me to bring back here. I was heartbroken to leave my kids and grandkids. We spent three years trying to go back to California, but that door was shut for good. I can see God's hand in bringing us back.

While we were in California GOD did so many huge miracles. Our track record for God doing the impossible was getting longer and longer and longer. Something I have come to lean on now, and the same goes for him... as the challenges are yet bigger, the miracles are even bigger yet.

I thought my marriage to this man would be "happily ever after". But GOD had different requirements of me than I thought would happen. My mate was not well. 'For better or worse' took on a new meaning. God had used me to take care of him, and in one instance, save his life.

He did the best he could, under the circumstances, but I was still trying to change him. Grapefruits will never be oranges! When I finally got that memo, it hit me hard! However, my hope is that God would intervene in this situation. Truth is, He was trying to change ME in the situation.

Oh, did I say that my husband is a believer of many

years with a strong love for his Beloved? We were NOT unequally yoked, as with the other relationships in my life. Being a Christian is determined by our fruit, not a name tag. My man was broken, not an unbeliever. Jesus was the glue holding us to Himself and each other.

Point #7: Do not yoke yourself with an unbeliever.

---

2 Corinthians 6:14 says, *"Do not be yoked together with unbelievers. For what do righteousness and wickedness have in common? Or what fellowship can light have with darkness?"* (NIV)

Believers are not perfect either! We are all struggling with our human condition. But knowing Jesus as Lord and Savior, is a leg up in troubled waters.

I am still on my journey with my man, and it has NOT turned out as I thought, or expected, or the way he thought. In 2012, he started losing his memory. That became the start of many diagnostic tests. We found out he had Asperger's Syndrome, a form of Autism. He was also ADHD, OCD, Passive Aggressive and Frontal Lobe Dementia was suspected, but still not confirmed. He also suffers from some personality disorders, cognitive issues, and emotional delay.

We still cannot explain the continuing memory loss. He described some childhood trauma and that explained some of the behavioral issues. The truth is, he could not have given me what I needed or wanted. He simply was not wired that way. But who knew? He had a huge servant's heart, childlike joy, and loved Jesus… still does.

We have an inseparable bond now and are dealing with a "new normal". I have had to wrap my head around the fact that I will never have the typical "normal' (that's a setting on the dryer) relationship in my life. I don't know the whole plan, but I can see that it was God taking care of both of us, the whole time, and He still is. My love for Dave comes out of the fact that he is valued for who he is, not what he does, or does not. God is challenging me to respect him, as he does, as a 'son of God'. Remember I said, God loves us just because we are! This is an amazing revelation.

My husband has limited understanding and it is a challenge to communicate occasionally. He has some mild cognitive issues as well. I guess I would say that God trusted me with His son, David.

Sometimes I feel I have failed him in not being stronger. However, I need to accept my own limitations as a human being, and setting healthy boundaries is ok. Let me say this, about that. We CAN change the dynamics in a relationship without trying to change the other person. When we change, they see the changes and will react to us accordingly. Please note the changes start with us!

When I made healthy boundaries, I ran the risk of things either getting worse or better. But something HAD to change, for sure. I did this with godly counsel and seeking God, myself. It did not turn out the way I thought, but the result was the best for both of us. Even David knew that. But God WAS working behind the scenes!

I seldom do things without Godly counsel. I have been on that end, and I'm tired of falling flat on my face. Some people are on a shorter leash than others. I am on a short leash with God. I'm fine with that. He has shown me He does know best.

When I ask the Lord how to pray for my husband, I sense it is that he would be kept happy and healthy.

My mate attempted to embrace his pain, and disabilities, and saw that he could not change, and voluntarily went to be properly cared for and supervised. He released me to do God's work, and he prays incessantly for me, and others. He is still trying to come to terms with his challenges.

Part of the challenge we have now is realizing that I

cannot fix him, and I am again learning how to deal with this 'new reality' when we see each other. The words "for better or worse, in sickness or in health" we spoke to each other on our wedding day, have really hit home for both of us. But David has agreed to our living arrangements, so it will not be too hard on either one of us. As he says in his chapter he "wanted the hurting to stop".

This is the short version of an ever evolving, very long story, and still I do not know where we are headed. God is still saying to me, "Keep your eyes on the white line," like the one in the storm. I am trusting Him that we are both committed to God, and whatever happens WILL BE for HIS Glory. So far, so good! I'll always hope and pray for healing for him, and as far as we are concerned God has healed our marriage. But not in the way we thought.

We will be married 25 years in April, 2018. Never in all of this, did I ever get release to leave my husband. I am committed, and he is, too. We are working out God's plan for our lives day by day. Sometimes, minute by minute.

At this point, and after many failures in his life, my husband embraced his limitations the best way he could and laid down his life for the Gospel and me. It is the way it says in Ephesians, Chapter 5. He put God's agenda and his wanting to make the 'hurting stop' toward me, a priority. He laid down his life for me and the Kingdom! He agreed to leave our home, but not our marriage. Myself, I was hurt, tired, and was starting to suffer physically from a prolonged time of stress. My body is healing! Thank you, Lord! David is my hero!

I am having to deal with the grief of broken dreams and expectations. There is that expectation thing again. But that is the issue. We all come with those expectations, and it can be so frustrating to the other mate. I have had to come to grips with living in separate places. But the time we do have together is filled with more quality than ever. No one is guaranteed tomorrow, so we both realize we need to treat each other in that vein.

Is it wrong to have dreams and expectations? I would say no. However, when those dreams and expectations are not centered on Him and what He wants for us, it can be a recipe as I said before, for crushing disappointments, and disaster. My husband and I both kept hearing in our spirits, 'Keep a light touch'. Neither of us knew at the time what that meant. We do now. For me right now, it means a prayer that goes something like this. "Lord, I know you can heal David at any time. I pray You do. I just want David to be happy. But please spare him of that awful mental condition, Dementia, if he indeed has it. I release him to You." That is the hardest prayer I have ever prayed.

When God calls us to serve, we just never know what that will entail. His grace toward us is not telling us more than we need to know. He knows our frame. If I had known all of this, I probably would have hidden under the bed.

It is ok to grieve those broken dreams and expectations. It's a process to get to the point of acceptance with hard realities. It comes in waves, and God is so gracious as not to let it overcome us. I have not stopped hoping, and it is walking the fine line between hope and reality; a very tricky line. But the journey has made me more sensitive to loving in a way I had not known possible.

Point #8: God is a jealous God and He wants all of us.

God is an out-of-the-box God. He has different solutions for all of us. But He does have solutions. He meets us at our individual place of need.

There was a fair amount of abuse toward me in this relationship in the past, but my husband's brokenness and diseases were the culprits here, not the person. God has given me great understanding as I was really stressed out about how to deal with his mental, neurological and developmental issues; they were quite worrisome. God took the decision out of my hands and worked out the solution, for both of us. It's amazing what God can do when we take our hands off and not take matters into our own hands. I did pray, and hard.

With all that has transpired between David and myself, we have peace and forgiveness and compassion towards each other that could not have happened any other way. God went that extra step with us. We were reconciled; each of us "owned' our own stuff. We also have a story to tell that hopefully will help someone else. God had the way of escape for both of us.

I cannot believe the change of heart in him, even though the symptoms of the illness are still present. My man said I have taught him tenacity. I say God has taught me how to love in ways unimaginable. But God's grace and love did abound to both of us. Isn't that what it is all about? At the end, when we stand before God, He will ask us, I am sure, "Did you learn how to love"? We can say without a doubt we have learned to love. I have often asked God, "Couldn't we have learned this another way?" He impressed on me that the degree of compassion, empathy and understanding that came from this, would cause a passion and drive to help others. The pain in these situations was a motivator to be a 'game changer' of the nth degree indeed!

I can tell there has been healing in my life because the abuses of the past no longer trigger emotions. I attribute that to forgiveness.

Point #9: God will bring about whatever we need in our lives to develop our character. He will orchestrate situations in our lives over and over until we get it, because He loves us. He is preparing us for heaven.

When we get to Heaven, I believe we are going to be asked if we have learned how to love. Learning that kind of love; to love like Him, may come with navigating moguls like this one.

Point #10: The grass IS NOT greener on the other side; it still needs to be mowed.

Our natural inclination in deep trials is to bolt and run. What would have happened if Jesus, knowing what was ahead of Him, said no to His Father's plan for our salvation? I am glad we don't have to find that out. He embraced His journey on our behalf, for the greater good. It is the fellowship of the intimacy of the sufferings of Jesus Christ, not something that is well preached. No one likes pain, but in Jesus' journey and through His pain and death, He entered into His full Sonship! After that, came the Resurrection Glory! I believe it is for us as well. Are you a hurting saint? Your glory may be just around the corner. You have entered into the fellowship of the intimacy of the sufferings of Jesus Christ! He tells us in scripture to pick up our 'crosses' and follow Him. Matthew 16:24 says Jesus never said we would not have trials or persecutions. He is looking to see what we will do with them. He is looking for overcomers.

We never know the full scope of how our pain and suffering can impact the Kingdom or others. We need to know that no matter what, Jesus is in our trials, and will never forsake us.

I'm so sorry it took me this long, and this many failures to get this memo! When God inspired me to write this book, He asked me to have my husband write the last chapter. He did, and it speaks for itself. I am a blessed woman, that he would bare his life to help others and hopefully inspire other men.

God is a bigger-picture God! We have limited and biased vision and perspective. That is a setup for disappointment. I have got that down pat.

Point #11: Failure is part of the learning curve; it is not an end in itself. Now that is a lesson in perspective we need to keep on our "hard drives."

Along with failure, usually comes fear; fear that one will make similar mistakes. That was probably why I never wanted to marry again, or even date, after journey number two.

Before I met David, my life with Jesus had taken a major leap forward, with total surrender to God. God was establishing a track record between us where I was able to experience Him like never before. I had come to trust Him in a way I never had before. By the time David was introduced to me, God had done a whole lot of healing in my life. In fact, I was at a point where I did not need a man, I wanted to share my life with David.

Fear is not from GOD. Please note there is also a difference between fear and caution. While caution says, proceed carefully and slowly, fear can often keep us from moving forward at all. Often fear is based on lies we believe about others, and ourselves. Fear: **F**alse **E**vidence **A**ppearing **R**eal; fear can immobilize us. How do you know the difference? You need to know the truth. God had done some amazing things to expose me to self-less men. I cannot say enough about how fear is a major assault weapon of the enemy. If you know the enemy's strategies, when those things come, you will know how to deal with them.

I was at a place in 1992 that I needed some additional finances, and the LORD heard my pleas and gave me a temporary job doing homecare for a couple from California that were here visiting. For the sake of anonymity, we will call them John and Jane. Jane was a quadriplegic from a terrible car accident. John married Jane, knowing all the care she would need. They were both spirit-filled Christians. I was in awe at this kind of love. God blessed their union in wonderful ways. She was even able to give him natural children. He knew GOD gave her to him, so she could be cared for. God was beginning to show me unusual circumstances, and sacrificial love in a marriage. He was also opening my heart to the fact that not all men had "issues."

As I said, we never know the full reasoning for what God calls us to. For myself, if I had known it all ahead of time, all that I would go through, my flesh would have run as fast as I could. But God knew His grace was on me in all of this, and as always, when He ordains something, He stays in the 'mix'. I could never say it was a mistake. Many encouraged me that it was, and I should give up. No, that was not what God was telling me. He protected and cared for both of us. Dave used to say, he was God's man on the job. I would dare say, we both were, and are!

Dave would often ask me if I would marry him again, knowing all I know now. I said yes. I knew that GOD had put us together. All the signs were there. God never said it would be easy, we thought it would be.

Again, things turned for me, when I just handed ALL of my life over to HIM. People used to laugh at me when I asked GOD to even invade the smallest details of my life. Why, I would get comments like, God gave you an intellect so use it." I would say back, "Yes, HE did and I am giving it back to Him. Look where it got me so far!" No reply.

On one of our trips to Colorado, our car had a transmission issue. I did not know it, but my husband came over to me with a bumper sticker. It said, "Faith makes things possible, but not easy." That is a great way to sum up our journey together!

I will say that there are times when abuse becomes a threat to our life or our children's lives. In that case, we need to make the correct decisions with counsel to move away from the abuser. There are no pat answers. However, I am trying to say that when we let GOD lead us, really make Him Lord of every area of our lives, He will be faithful to complete what He started in us, no matter how bad it looks at the moment.

Also, please don't think we have it all together. There are still emotions involved from living separately, one of which is having to embrace the fact that our marriage will not be what either one of us had envisioned or expected. There are plenty of other challenges, too. But we know for sure how much God loves each one of us, and that OUR marriage healing came in this way. I also know because of some circumstances, God is using us in a stealth-like fashion where we are planted now for a greater good. We do know that we are in the center of His will, as odd as it may seem.

One of my man's comments to me was that he has had healing in his life. He had many rejection and abandonment issues. He is finally convinced that I am loyal, committed and tenacious towards him and our marriage. It has also been a witness to others in how we are conducting ourselves in this. He thanks me over and over for being his advocate, and for not bailing on him.

Both of us have learned many things we would have never learned another way. My man often says to me, "I don't know what tomorrow brings, but I know WHO holds tomorrow." Indeed!

He prays for me and others like never before. He can no longer drive because of his physical disabilities, or perform his past occupations, but he has found a heavenly purpose. He is a light that shines in dark places.

I can tell when I am with him, his heart is in a great place, and I am so grateful for that.

When we are together, peace reigns. There is no more of the unhealthy anger; just thankfulness, love, respect, honor, and treating each other like tomorrow would be our last day. Things get resolved quickly. God loves us too much to leave us the way we were. He will go to great lengths to perfect us.

One of the things that confused me was all the great WORDS spoken over us. I had a revelation that was confirmed by two pastors. It was that time for the believer to move forward from glory to–glory. Life everlasting. There is a new millennium coming. God does hasten His word to preform it. Even in the next step in the Kingdom, we will not be married, but WORDS spoken now, that do not get fulfilled, I believe will be when Jesus comes back and establishes His government here on earth.

Forgiveness

Forgiveness keeps our hands clean and allows the Lord into the situation with the other person. The way I read the bible it is NOT an option, nor is it a feeling. Forgiveness is a decision. The Bible tells us that God forgives us, and we must forgive others. The Bible also says if we don't forgive, we are not forgiven.

"In prayer there is a connection between what God does and what you do. You can't get forgiveness from God, for instance, without also forgiving others. If you refuse to do your part, you cut yourself off from God's part." Matthew 6:14-15 (MSG)

Let us address how love releases forgiveness. Luke 7:44-48 says, *"Then He turned to the woman and said to Simon, "Do you see this woman? I entered your house; you gave Me no water for My feet, but she has washed My feet with her tears and wiped them with the hair of her head. You gave Me no kiss, but this woman has not ceased to kiss My feet since the time I came in. You did not anoint*

My head with oil, but this woman has anointed My feet with fragrant oil. Therefore, I say to you, her sins, which are many, are forgiven, for she loved much. But to whom little is forgiven, the same loves little. Then He said to her, "Your sins are forgiven."

What the Lord showed me about this passage, with special attention to verse 47, was that when we don't forgive others, we hinder their ability to love. We can also say, whomever is forgiven much, will love much. In addition, we are no longer in right standing with God. If we do not forgive, we are disobedient. Is it possible that we can be a hindrance if we live in unforgiveness toward others, preventing them from reaching their potential in love? When we forgive it does not negate the offender's actions, it is a release for us, and them. One other thing I find fascinating about this passage is her active love for Him that released Jesus to forgive her sins. She did not formally ask for forgiveness.

The parable before this one about the debtors, also indicates that compassion drove the person they were indebted to, to also forgive their debt. All they did was say that they could not pay.

Forgiveness is an amazing force in releasing others and ourselves. It also releases the power of God in circumstances we may deem impossible. There is a lie most people believe that says the offending person is getting off scott-free if we forgive. It is actually the opposite. Forgiving does not mean we have to like what happened, or that we have to live in that situation. Also, forgiveness is a decision and act of our will, not of our emotions.

One of the other things worth noting is forgiveness is not complete if we are angry at ourselves. We must also forgive ourselves, most often for bad decisions or choices we have made. Once we lay them at the cross, God forgives us. Our sin is wiped out.

The enemy of our souls is always looking for an open door to dismantle what God is doing with us. Frequently an attack on us comes in through offense, bitterness or unforgiveness. Staying in that vein not only puts static on our spiritual line, but I have seen the effects on the physical body as well. When we don't forgive, it is implied we are in judgement as well. The Bible says we are not to judge others either.

Let's us now talk about forgiveness vs. reconciliation. Sometimes, we forgive, but there seems to be no closure. Sometimes we cannot talk to the other person. I had this experience with my second husband. I had an order of protection and I was not allowed to talk to him. But I did have to forgive him. Eventually, I knew the forgiveness was complete when I thought of or spoke of the painful things and there were no longer strong emotions that accompanied the thought.

I really appreciated the movie, "*The Shack*" by William P. Young[1], based off the book written by the Canadian author, published in 2007 by Windblown Media. Although there were many biblical overtures throughout, the theme I want to focus on was forgiveness and God's love. God allowed all sorts of experiences to come to the main character, Mack, to allow him to forgive his dad, who had abused him. Once he saw, and acted on that forgiveness, he was able to reconcile the pain of loss in his own life and move on. He saw that God was in all the hard places, and did indeed love him, and had never left him in his life journey.

This movie was a powerful allegory! Hard things do happen to good people. Further on in the movie, Mack was reconciled allegorically to his natural dad, and God was able to show Mack that his own father had been abused. Case in point, as I said early on, the propensity and learned behavior of abuse had been carried on. Mack's dad did not abuse Mack intentionally. It was all he knew. But the redemptive force of God prevailed. Again, you cannot get orange juice from a grapefruit. But moving forward in the movie, the cycle of abuse ended with Mack.

---

[1] Young, William P.; Motion Picture Artwork ©; 2016; Summit Entertainment, LLC. All rights reserved.

Though it does not always work like this, God is on the move with His people in redemptive ways. We all will be given choices. God's heart is preparing us for eternity and He will do what needs to be done to get out all those spots and wrinkles that the Bible talks about. I am convinced that in the end, when we stand before our Maker, He is going to ask us, "Did you learn how to love?" The journey to love God's way is different for all of us. Do we see God's perspective in some of our trials? Maybe not, but maybe now we will be looking for it.

Also, the author was trying to convey that we ALL have "shacks" in our lives we need to deal with. These shacks are the no-fly zones that we erect when pain arises. Sometimes those shacks need to be confronted and visited for closure, especially if it keeps us from advancing spiritually.

Once Mack faced his shack, and was able to forgive, he finally found closure. God had pursued him, and to me it demonstrated how important the power of forgiveness is, and how important it is to God.

In another video the author describes that in order for reconciliation to take place, the offending party had to own their mistakes. That can be helpful, but it is not always possible. However, forgiveness is a mandate in His word, and we may be holding our own deliverance captive if we don't forgive those who have hurt us. Reconciliation though, requires participation by the other person. Forgiveness is a given, but reconciliation may not always be possible. One can always aspire to and pray for reconciliation.

Matthew, Chapter 6 says:

"Pray, then, in this way: 'Our Father who is in heaven, Hallowed be Your name. 'Your kingdom comes. Your will be done, on earth as it is in heaven. 'Give us this day our daily bread. 'And forgive us our debts, as we also have forgiven our debtors. 'And do not lead us into temptation but deliver us from evil. For Yours is the kingdom and the power and the glory forever. Amen.'

For if you forgive others for their transgressions, your heavenly Father will also forgive you. But if you do not forgive others, then your Father will not forgive your transgressions." (NASB)

Finally, let us discuss breaking ungodly soul ties. After my second husband left, I continued to have terrible nightmares about him. A Christian sister advised me to pray and ask the Lord to break any and all ungodly soul ties. I did and the nightmares stopped.

Even in some situations, while still in difficult relationships we can ask the LORD to break any ungodly soul ties with that individual. It is very powerful and will free us up in many ways, in and out of a hard situation.

Not Just My Story!

Many men and women have traveled this road. Although most of the following testimonies do not have all the details of their journeys, I know my sisters that shared, had very hard roads. All these women are amazing testimonies of God's redemptive work and overcoming power. I love that their focus is on how GOD's grace carried them through. That is where the power is! They confronted the enemy of their souls with one of the greatest weapons available to us, forgiveness!

Point #12: Success is not always measured in getting the result we want. It's in the overcoming.

Preliminary comments I received about my journey demonstrated Jesus to certain people. God and I have never agreed on what I think I can handle. But He knows my frame well. I wish sometimes we would not have to go through a literal hell to make a strong message and witness. But can you agree that those are the ones we most likely will remember? God DOES know what HE is doing, and He knows who to hand out the tough assignments to!

I pray that you are blessed by the following testimonies. Each woman was asked three questions and responded with limited information based on the difficulty of the subject matter. The questions were:

1) Were you abused, and if so, what type of abuse did you incur?

2) How did having Jesus in your life help you in your journey?

3) What kind of advice would you give to someone in a similar journey that might help them?

Please note: To date, all of these women are serving God, thriving, and happy. Was it an easy journey? I don't know, but the common thread I saw in all five testimonies was they allowed Jesus to be Lord of their lives, forgive their mistakes, lean on Him to part their Red Sea's, and to carry them across to that abundant life they now enjoy. To God be the Glory.

See for yourself! *"With God all things are possible!"* Matthew 19:26d

Testimony # 1

In 1 Corinthians 10:13 we find that God promises, *"He will provide a way of escape."* Do you remember going through a fire drill in school or at your work place? Have you considered having one at home, especially if you have children? It is something to think about.

How about one for your day to day life?

Living in a broken world, as we all do in one way or another, finding the way of escape is not only critical for your survival, but also for your spiritual/emotional health and well-being.

1 Peter 5:8 warns us... *"Stay alert! Watch out for your great enemy, the devil. He prowls around like a roaring lion, looking for someone to devour."*

It is easy to bury our heads in the sand, the TV or the cell phone and suddenly find ourselves attacked. We are wired to quickly defend ourselves and counter attack... or to run. We usually identify the source of the attack as the person we see in the natural.

As a woman living in a home, married to a man who was physically stronger than I was, I found myself often in a position where defending myself with a verbal "counter attack," put me in a position that if tempers escalated, it potentially opened up the opportunity for physical responses.

Identifying a way of escape became critical. In the early years, I would retreat and "go scrub the tub." In more difficult times, I made sure my purse and car keys were always in a specific place and would run out the door and leave. Depending on the degree of the confrontation, I would call by cell phone and discuss at a safe distance.

What I didn't realize in the heat of the battles then, was who my enemy really was. The enemy prowls around in many ways, but he is not a person. When Jesus said to Peter, *"Get behind me, Satan,"* He may have appeared to be speaking to Peter directly, but we know he was actually speaking to "The Influencer." Our enemy is not our spouse. Our spouse may have opened the door to the wrong Influencer...or in some cases I may have allowed wrong thinking to influence me. There are times we all need solitude and safety and then sometimes we need "marching orders".

Escaping from the evil one's influence led me to the arms of God. In discussions with my heavenly Father, He reminded me in Psalm 23 *"He prepares a **table** before me in the presence of my enemies."* I should meditate on that.

What is on the table? It became a Table of Meeting. What was on The Table changed every day; sometimes there were "battle plans," sometimes there were "love gifts;" sometimes a feast, sometimes manna and water.

What's on your Table today as you spend time with the Lord? Plan a way of escape... and retreat to The Table.

Thanks be to my Loving, Gracious, Compassionate, and Victorious Father God.

Testimony #2

I would love to share a few thoughts of what I have learned in my 30+ year relationship with the Lord. Above all, He is Faithful. He will never leave you or forsake you. It seems so simple, but it took me a long time to actually believe it and to know in my innermost being who God is.

I was lost, and He found me, and what I didn't know at that time was that He had always been with me. I was lost in sin, lost to drugs, and utterly lost in destructive relationships. Jesus has showed Himself to be Faithful in every aspect of my life. He took this broken, lost woman and showed me what love, joy, peace, patience, kindness, goodness, faithfulness, gentleness, and self-control are. Now, I would like to say that learning to produce these fruits in me and through me was easy, but the lessons of God are tough and sometimes those lessons even hurt, but like gold refined in the fire, they brought forth something that is priceless; Christ in me (and you) the Hope of Glory!

I would like each one of you to know that you can trust God. Even if you can't see the answer, stand firm in faith. Believe the Word and be in the Word of God each and every day. Always love one another. Learn how to hear what the Lord is saying to you and then trust Him with that word. Stop making those decisions that you know are wrong, just to please others. God loves you and wants to bless you. I want to encourage you to be the woman of God that you were made to be; strong and happy, despite what the world says.

Testimony # 3

First, I want to give a gentle reminder... we are ALL BROKEN! When we recognize that, it points us to Jesus, the only One that can help us; His Hand extended so we can hold on, bringing strength and encouragement to us in whatever situation we are in.

Ever hear the James Taylor song, *"You've Got a Friend"*? It reminds us that when we are down and troubled and simply need a helping hand—when it feels like we are in our 'darkest night', that we've got a friend? The one that says we can simply close our eyes and think of that friend, and He'll be there?

That song perfectly describes the place in my life and

heart that I try to put Jesus - through good times and bad. Everything Jesus is, lives inside me through His Spirit, when I recognize that, HE IS ALWAYS there. When you go through difficulties, especially with someone you love, there is no "magic formula" or 1, 2, 3 step to get a certain result.

What does help is knowing HE relates to us as individuals, and on a personal level. HE WILL ALWAYS HELP US IN A WAY WE CAN UNDERSTAND AND RELATE TO.

I am a very 'feeling' type of person; I feel what someone else is going through. So when I go through a difficult situation, I can become very emotional and my feelings tend to 'lead' me. In any difficult situation, it's important that God's Word does the leading—not our feelings. Feelings will usually mislead us. Find something He says works for you. For me, I stood on scripture that reminded me He was with me, helping me.

"Thanks be to God who leads us in Triumph."

"The Lord is my Shepherd; He leads me beside STILL WATERS."

"If you faint in the day of adversity, your strength is small."

And most importantly, for me, because I love music

and worship, I know that as I worship, He fights for me!

There are so many things I could say, but I will conclude with a story I told my sons when they were little boys, about faith and trusting in a God we can't see with our eyes – but who is ALWAYS THERE. Here is what I told them:

"Pretend you are standing on a high ledge, at the edge, facing backwards so you can't see how far up you are. While you are standing there, a voice [God] speaks to you and says, "Fall backwards and I will catch you...."

You look around and don't see anyone, and you hear the voice again saying the same thing. "Trust me," you hear. So, you take a step and fall backwards focusing only on those words, "I'll catch you." And you feel strong arms reach out to catch you, and you hear the words, "I love you."

In that moment, you realize you can trust Him – truly in good times and hard times, "You've got a friend."

Testimony #4

My first husband was already broken when I married him. It was a bitter, long, drawn-out divorce. Before that, he was abused by a mother who is bipolar, and used him to take out her aggression on. As with any marriage, it started out with romance and fun. But then his hardened heart and bitterness took over. I became the person that he emotionally threw up on, and was the battering ram for his hurt. Because he could not love himself, he certainly could not love me the way I needed.

When I got to the end of myself, and in my darkest moment, I cried out to the Lord with all my heart. I asked him to change my husband, but He changed me first. My heart needed to be healed. I needed to look to Jesus, instead of looking to anyone else.

This is how God healed me: I learned to praise Him in the storm. I learned to pray His Word. I learned to trust Him. I learned to cry out to Him, first. I learned a gentle answer turns away wrath. I learned to serve my husband instead of demanding to be served. I learned to worship Him in dance; I learned to be honest with myself. I learned that God hears the cry of our hearts. I learned that God has us in His hands. At the end of our life together, God will have transformed me.

Testimony # 5

I have been abused pretty much my whole life. I was picked on all of my life! Some people laughed and made jokes about me, yelled at me, tortured me by the things they said that were very hurtful. I have been called so many things to my face that were not nice at all or that were far from the truth. I was tiny for my age and people had a good time at my expense. My parents were not the happiest people in life, due to their upbringing. I felt that my Mother hated me, all the time, and to this day I still feel that way. I have tried to make her happy so that she would want to love me. My Dad was an alcoholic and he was miserable and probably hated himself. My parents had 4 children and I am the oldest. Life wasn't always the sweetest.

I developed very low self-esteem and self-worth. I tried my very hardest to do everything right, so I wouldn't get in trouble. I also became a perfectionist and developed OCD! I have been manipulated pretty much my whole life. I had a husband that abused me mentally, emotionally, physically and sometimes sexually. He also tried to kill me a few times. He continued to tell me I was not even worth the space I took up; that everybody hates me. People don't want anything to do with me and they want to be left alone!!!

One night, after one of these conversations took place, I was getting ready to take a shower and get ready for bed. When I got in the shower, I was crying and asking God, "Why am I alive if I am this horrible and not worth the space I take up?" This was a turning point in my life!! God heard me!!!

I had been going to church since I was a little girl. I asked Jesus into my heart and life when I was in high school!! I heard from people that I was a "Bible thumper"!! I thought I was a Christian!! I enjoyed being able to go to church and Bible study. I was old enough to drive and I had a friend from high school that went with me.

When people criticize you and give you a hard time and you are already an emotional wreck, it's not easy. I wasn't in God's Word strongly, so I wavered. I knew God was My Savior and He loved me!! God has brought beautiful, special people into my life to encourage me and inspire me to share the beauty of my soul!!!

After praying in the shower that night, God sent me blessings of encouragement and love from people. I started to feel that maybe I was OKAY!! Don't worry! The ENEMY was attacking me every chance he had!!! I can't tell you how many have lied about me saying things that I have never said or done. It destroyed so many friendships and humiliated me in front of others. They have tried to destroy my work ethic to supervisors and they were believed!! The list goes on!! Judgement day will come for ALL of US!!!

I prayed to God to please make me the Christian women he wants me to be!!! God has brought magnificent and awesome people into my life. God has healed me and cleansed me and I have seen myself go to the cross and lay all of my baggage, hurt and garbage down, and the darkness in my life leave!! I feel like I could float since I have been cleansed. I see the white light and I FEEL GOD'S LOVE FLOWING OUT OF ME WITH SUCH JOY AND HAPPINESS!!! I am praising and thanking God for his amazing love, mercy and grace He gives in His Precious Holy Life!!! You can feel this, too! Trust in Jesus!!! He is waiting for YOU!! Amen!!

Love to all of you!!! You are precious and wonderful!! This is the first time in my whole life that I can say I love me!!!!! Alleluia!!! It is the most wonderful feeling EVER!!!

David's Story

My name is David. I am 58 years old at this writing. I am what I call a recovering passive aggressive (PA). I use the term PA when referring to the person I used to be when I married Josephine. I did not know I was a PA.

In 2012, I started having memory issues and we did all sorts of testing. I also found out I had Asperger's, which is a form of Autism, as well as OCD, ADHD, Passive Aggressive and some personality disorders. I was also tested for Frontal Lobe Dementia. It didn't take long to see our marriage was in trouble.

Now it's the end of 2016, and I'm writing this. At my age, it is humbling to learn that most of our problems were my fault. We had been married at this time for 23 years.

As it was explained to me, the combination of all these conditions, minus the dementia, is very troubling and each condition exacerbates the other. It seems as though the PA was the worst. I also had been traumatized as a child, and as a result, had formed other personality problems. Even the doctor, a neuro psychologist, said he had "never seen anything like this before."

When I learned about this situation in 2012, I felt God softened my heart to prepare me to receive correction. Prior to that, I was too proud to learn I had problems.

My lack of education has hurt me a great deal. In high school, I went to BOCES. I see this now as a big mistake. I had been conditioned to believe that men should work, provide for their families, etc., either just out of or actually still in high school. So, while still in high school, I worked at a local hardware store. I was hired to fix lawn mowers, but the guy fixing appliances quit, so I was handed a service call on a refrigerator problem. I ordered the parts and fixed it. That made me the appliance guy, too.

When I graduated high school, I kept working at the hardware store. In those years I also was busy restoring a Camaro, causing me to miss out on social activities. I dated some girls, but they never let me know I was broken. When I look back, I can see how I was self-absorbed. I had some friends, but not what I would call bosom friends — you know what I mean.

I tell you this, my testimony, to show you my mistakes. I don't want sympathy. My wife has taught me what tenacity is.

I am grateful to Cathy Meyer, a Certified Divorce Coach, Marriage Educator and Legal Investigator, for writing *"What Kind of Woman Marries a Passive Aggressive Man?"* [2] This article changed my life. Cathy Meyer has written many articles about PA. She was married to one for a while. She divorced him.

As Christians, there are not many Scriptural reasons to divorce. I was conditioned into service work. Christianity was good for me, I tried to give people what they wanted. I read where marriage was work. I tried to fold this idea into marriage. I was consumed with work, as you might guess.

Growing up, I watched Star Trek on TV. I related to Leonard Nemoy's character, *Mr. Spock*, the man with no emotions. In other words, I heard about feelings, but I knew not what they were. I knew what anger was. I used it a plenty. Anger might be a motivator, but rarely makes friends. I've be very angry and then answer the phone normally. This told me that anger is a choice, or it was with me.

Now, I choose a better way. My wife, before I read Cathy's paper, would refer to, "Dave's, Bless Me

---

[2] Meyer, Cathy, (2017, September 24, 2nd edition). *What Kind of Woman Marries the PA Man?* Retrieved from https://www.liveabout.com/what-kind-of-woman-marries-the-passive-aggressive-man-1102897.

Club." She told me this many times. You see, a PA man is programmed to receive. My wife was full of love. The more she gave love, the more I rejected it. I did not really know how to give it. I was and am a "romantic clod." So, her referring to the "Dave's, Bless Me Club", was the only way she could say it. But even as good and expressive as my wife is, I was way too proud to receive it. A PA man blames others for the way things are, or the problems we face.

In another Cathy Meyer paper, she said the only hope for a PA man is if he can look internally, not externally, for reasons to problems. He needs to face his childhood fears, not to be right, but to be open to a better way. A nephew of mine referred to "narcissistic personalities." I've thought a lot about his statement. He is a teacher by occupation. You see, I was too proud even then, to see my own folly. I had not only had to quit doing the don'ts, I had to do the do's. To this day, I have trouble with relationships. You see, I've tried to make some changes. Sure, I tried to quit the revenge, the back biting, and the rest of the inappropriate behaviors that PA guys do.

I know a few women who are PA, too. I pray for them and their spouses.

My wife is on fire for God. She also has a grateful heart, even being married to me. She, to me, is a remarkable woman. I like the way she writes; it's sort of like she's talking to you. Wow! That's a gift from God.

I've seen other people who watch TV 'hyper focused'. I am that way, but not because I want to be. I watch TV hoping to learn a better way of life.

I am grateful for "Feeling Lists." A while back we attended a marriage seminar. The book they gave us had a list of pleasant feelings on the front inside cover, and unpleasant feelings on the back inside cover. That book helped me more than I can say; I learned how to identify and express my feelings.

As I said before, a PA person can still be PA, but nicer about it. Quit the lying, too. With me, I lied about things, hoping for a better reality. It never worked. And one gets labeled a liar. The Bible says, *"All liars will have their part in the Lake of Fire"* (Author's paraphrase). That scared the bejeebers out of me. I didn't even realize the lies. I pray for people who are married to liars.

I am sorry to ramble on and on. Many people have tried to help me. But God opened my eyes to see how my PA was hurting them. I finally saw my own faults. I didn't want to be a liar. And I was. Cathy Meyer wrote of many real-life points. She had to have lived it. She helped me more than I can say.

I am no longer a liar. Although, I was always true to

my wife, to this day she has trouble trusting me. One cannot trust a PA man. A good man says what he means and means what he says. There you go. For years I wrote the words, but rarely followed through on "means what he says." By that definition I am not trustworthy.

My father always told me, "Tell them [women] what they want to hear and do what you want to do." That's a terrible way to raise a child. That was me. An irresponsible man gets angry a lot, thinking he will get attention. It's a stupid way to treat a lady.

Guys, get this nugget. You are responsible for your anger. You are responsible for your spouse. She is a gift from God. God is not happy with an angry man. I've been there. No one likes an angry man. Enough of that. Many of you know these things. It's taken me most of my life to learn them. It's my fault; my bad.

Young men, get an education. I did use geometry in air conditioning work. There you go. Things you learned in school, you do use in adulthood. They might seem ridiculous now, but learn them. God will use them. You will see.

In closing, anger is a lousy servant. Women don't like angry guys. I can't say enough about anger. Get a hold of it now, or it will control you. Choose a better way. That was me. The rest of you might need a time out. Talk to your lady. In an argument, a time out might be an answer to quality time with your spouse. Give her your best; it will pay off in many ways. Your spouse should be your best friend, or your spouse will go elsewhere. *"You picked a fine time to leave me, Lucille."*[3] That was his fault. He wasn't giving her his best. She got scraps and she got tired of waiting. We guys get spaced out and miss it: a lot. And the disenchanted wife goes elsewhere, and it's our fault. A wife wants closeness, cooperation, love, and attention. She wants to hear that he loves her every day. Some women need lots of reassurance. It's not a 'got that done' kind of thing. Correction, I will say most women need to hear it a lot.

Thank you for hearing my heart. Again, not a 'poor me' kind of thing. We are a summation of our choices. Let your wife know, when she's calm, about your needing a time out. I've been there, when the wife follows you around, letting you know you can't quit on this conversation. But you might want the time out. Tell her, then come back in ten minutes. An understanding female will let you go. They want to connect. The time out at one time in my life was a God send. For me, now I choose a different way. When I was younger, I didn't really understand feelings.

There are Scriptures that blessed me through these

---

[3] Bowlinger, Roger & Bynum, Hal; United Artists, Recorded by Kenny Rogers;1977.

years.

I Peter 3:15,16 (KJV) says, *"But sanctify the Lord God in your hearts; and always be ready to give an answer to every man that asketh you a reason of the hope that is in you with meekness and fear; having a good conscience; that whereas they speak evil of you, as of evildoers, they may be ashamed that falsely accuse your good conversation in Christ."* (KJV)

I want to explain where I am with respect to my wife at present.

My handicaps, as I've come to know them, can be destructive to myself and others. My dysfunction has hurt my wife. I have done impulsive and dangerous things. I do not want to hurt her anymore, or have her worry about me, when she is away in ministry. I've obtained other living arrangements. Hopefully, so she could do her travelling without worrying about her 'broken husband'. She sees me as a loose cannon in her words. I am.

In the meantime, I've tried to make strides in leaving my passive aggressive personality. I've also learned I cannot just *not* do the don'ts; I do have to *do* the do's, scripturally. This is a mouthful, but the Lord does have some instructions in the book of Ephesians. As a man, to put on Christ… I see this as a lifelong pursuit. Galatians is another book that has ministered to me through the years. Know the Word and do it. As you all know, as James says, "Do it, now!" and "Lord, it's me again. Help!!" A prayer I've used a lot, when I don't like who I am, is, "Can a man change his personality?" I think there are times when God looks at us to do the work, but when we do, God is there to help. I love the Lord for being a personal Savior. He is there in our time of need.

Well, having said all that, He never said it would be easy. Well, maybe He did, *"Come unto me ye who are weary and learn of Me, and I will give you rest. My yoke is easy and my burden is light."* My paraphrase of Mathew 11:28. *(KJV)*

So, we guys have hope. We learn we disciples are in a war. Our enemy is as a 'roaring lion.' "Yeah, he might roar but he has no teeth!" For me, it was the TV and is the TV. I look at whether it is edifying. We must shut off the smut. The TV controlled me. I heard or saw nothing that was going on around me. From a Christian perspective, we should be ever vigilant, integral. I don't know about you, but for me, I see Gods handiwork in creation. I also see how Satan is into TV. He has been around a long time; he knows how to attack us effectively. Let us read God's instruction book, the Bible.

Proverbs has a lot of applicable truths. If you don't read them, you have no excuse. Hebrews 9:27 says, *"It is appointed once to die and then the judgement."* *(KJV)*

One does not want to get there before the appointed time. And we are not given this time. He says do not kill, especially yourself. We will have to give account for what we did with what we were given.

For me, this is sobering. I hope it is sobering to you, too. We are called to live for Him; to be about His business, His purpose and goals. If you are lacking purpose for your life, guys, look at your family; your first ministry. I've made a mess of mine. My testimony is full of regrets; I screwed up my family. I am the youngest of six; one brother, four sisters. My mother, God rest her soul, she hated my wife. I could have married Raquel Welch and it wouldn't have made a difference. But I had my part in pitting them against her. I was a people pleaser.

My Dad died in 1980. Before that, I moved back home when Dad got sick. I lived ten years with my Mom. Mom transferred Dad's responsibilities to me. I didn't see it at the time, but that's what happened. So, when I got over my first marriage in 1984-85, I married my wife Josephine in 1993. To Mom, the man left the house, not "David finally got a life.". Mom had some hang ups there, and she shared her feelings with all who would listen. At the time, I could not change her mind. I hoped God showed her 'her twisted thinking'. I have one sister; we grew up together. I made the mistake of trusting her. She betrayed my trust.

So, my siblings don't like my wife because she has a prophetic gift. She says it is like it is. Prophetic people aren't often liked by outsiders. This is what it is; my family didn't really like my father. I feel he also had a prophetic gift. He often said it like it is. This often came back to bite dad.

By my testimony, I hope it helps you with some of your struggles. For me, it's hard to love someone who thinks you stink. I do pray for them. I've heard God gives you friends; the devil gives you your relatives. And for me, I've made my bed. Sure, I have regrets. I created many of our problems. I've been gullible and it bit me in the butt; that was hard.

I tell you this not to bellyache, but I know firsthand how hard family relationships are, and how gossip gets out of hand. I am an example of how some things go astray, and not everyone is for you. God says the godly will suffer persecution, a promise that I have seen.

My mother-in-law was a mother I didn't have. She was as remarkable as her daughter is. You see, for Josephine and me, opposites attracted. I hope you can glean something from my messed-up life, a sad example of a gutless man. But I trust He can take my mess and make it a message of what not to do. My example is how God works in a marriage, for better or worse. I've had the worse. I hope the better will last.

It will be a time when the wife is satisfied by the husband. Our God works in very strange ways. I wanted to share some good things that God has done for us!

This is all from David's pen. Amen. More thoughts....

For the mystery of God has been shown to us in His Word, if we would read it and do it, we would be changed. Ephesians 4:31-32 has ministered to me a lot. We need to put on the New Man, after Christ. Verses 31 and 32 say, *"Let all bitterness and wrath and anger and clamor and evil speaking be put away from you; with all malice."* *Be ye kind one to another, tenderhearted, forgiving one another even as God for Christ's sake forgave you."*

And adding to that Ephesians 6:10 or 5:25. For me, that 5:25 scripture speaks to married men; it says, *"Husbands, love your wives, even as Christ loved the church and gave Himself for it."* With me, applying these Scriptures is a lifelong project. Yeah, Christ should be in your heart unto good works. Applying these Scriptures and the ones following helped. Ephesians 5:24 says, *"Therefore, as the church is subject to Christ..."*. There is more to that verse but I find it interesting. The men are counselled to love their wives, but the wives are not commanded to love their husbands; only respect them. There it is.

If we guys get it right, then your wife will automatically love you. Funny how that works in God's Kingdom. Okay, these are hard words for us, guys. When you are unemployed in our culture, how does that work? Through the washing with the water of the Word. Are you reading Scripture to your wife? There's no time like the present. It doesn't say if you're broken, you are exempt. That whole fourth and fifth chapter of Ephesians is a very good read. Underline verse 25 in the fifth chapter of Ephesians.

I have a study Bible with all the Greek and Hebrew words for the works of the flesh and the fruit of the Spirit defined. It's a very interesting read. We guys like to apply ourselves. Or I do. If any of you guys are told you are controlling, I have a list for you.

1. Be vulnerable with people.
2. Never compromise your self-respect by altering your core beliefs.
3. Be realistic about your expectations of others.
4. Quit the passive aggressive nonsense. Be real with people, and your expectations.
5. We men put on masks with people. I know I've used the absent-minded professor routine.
6. More on being real:
   a. These things are hard to implement, but have we put on Christ?
   b. Have you put off the works of the flesh? I am fascinated that the works of the

flesh mentioned in Galatians includes hatred. It says we are to judge ourselves. The fruit of the spirit is a package deal. We find this in Galatians 5:19. Hatred is listed, along with adultery and fornication, idolatry, and witchcraft. I've had to go to God in prayer about this one. In every sense, we are to keep our spirit clear. Hatred and malice will not inherit the Kingdom of God. Many times, hatred is listed with idolatry and witchcraft. We ought not to do these things. The Holy Ghost wrote these things to us. If we don't read it, we are without excuse.

More on hatred.... one cannot like everyone, but we must not wrestle with hatred. I don't like my sisters and brother. But I don't hate them. There is a difference.

If we hate people we can lose our salvation; those are loaded words. Now I see Christ in the book of Revelation... hating the deeds of the Nicolaitans. I think the real issue here is Jude: 20-23.... hating the garment spotted with the flesh. I do like that whole stance. Verse 21 says to keep yourself in the love of God.... looking for the mercy of our Lord Jesus Christ unto eternal life.

Verses 22-23 say, *"And of some have compassion making*

a difference.... others save with fear, pulling them out of the fire; hating the garment spotted by the flesh." Flesh — spelled backwards is h-self: h for his or her. Whatever towel you use, it is self-centered. I've stumbled over these verses. I've read commentaries, but the rendering is that way for a reason. Guys, get a hold of these verses. There is a difference between hatred and hating. So, its ok to hate the works of the flesh. But we must be careful not to harbor hatred. There is an awful fruit for our labor. So, we come away with, stay away from hatred!!! It's ok to hate the garment spotted by the flesh. And to hate the deeds of the Nicolatians in Revelation 2:16. The answer... repent! The sword of His mouth. There we are. It scares me. I hope I don't harbor hatred. There is a fine line there; could be why Jesus says love your enemies....

OK, the Spirit says to love your enemies. Do them good. Stay away from hatred, except when it's a deed of the flesh. So, there we are.... judge scripture with Scripture.

Matthew 5, 6 and part of 7 is all about the Sermon on the Mount. Jesus had a lot to teach us here. Boy, did I get off on a tangent again. I wanted some encouragement for men; I've hit some meaty Scriptures. We have a God that will work with us in applying His Truths.

He will help us to bless our wives and not harm them. Philippians 4:13 says, *"I can do all things according to His purpose and goals, in His riches and glory."* There we go. He gives us the plan and works in us to do His good pleasure. He will help us. There we are. Guys, stay out of anger and hatred. Those two top things I fight for every day. Who wouldn't want to bless his wife....as Christ did the church? Those are honorable pursuits.

I love the King James Bible. An idea... put 3 ribbons in your Bible...1 ribbon cycles you through the Old Testament, one ribbon does Psalms and Proverbs, and the 3rd ribbon does the New Testament. I personally don't do all my ribbons every day because some passages are meaty and I spend more time in one ribbon and then the others are slower. I don't do a reading schedule. I think some passages need more attention: Leviticus for one and 1 Corinthians for another.

I think a good Christian should read the Word to be unspotted from the world. Guys, these are nuggets. I want to end with a paper my wife gave me: *25 Ways to Love Your Wife* [4]...... its practical.

---

[4] Flanders, Douglas. The Prodigy Project; www.Flandersfamily.info.

1. Listen to your wife. Look into your wife's eyes. And truly listen, intently! What she says can be a surprise to you.
2. Communicate....be a positive thinker. Don't make her guess what you are thinking or feeling.
3. Sing her praises. I've dropped this ball in my own life, but brag about her to your friends.
4. Intimacy is a two-way street. If you make this area a priority, it pays off other ways. My folks were sexually active right through my father's death. They didn't get a whole lot right, but I saw they truly loved each other and held each other close all my teen years.
5. Pray for her and with her...this puts her needs at the keel of your mind where they should be.
6. Value her for who she is; guys get this one right. Value her as you would yourself. Galatians 5. It pays off in other ways.
7. Put the toilet seat down. This might sound like a simple thing that we miss, but....
8. Turn off the TV....do a board game instead; we like chess, this always has a winner and a loser.
9. Put your clothes in the hamper...don't let her think she is your maid. The hamper is not far away from where you take them off, so do this. It will pay off in numerous ways. Help with the laundry. My wife spins so many plates. I am happy to do something for her.

10. Loose the purse strings...we all keep an eye on the budget, but let her have some once in a while. An occasional splurge can recharge her batteries; not to mention yours.

11. Cut out the conversation of our culture, your quick wit can be the life of the party or a pain in the neck. I've learned to bite my tongue in this area especially.

12. Set some cave time for her. We all need some time to ourselves, but make together time.

13. Be careful with female friendships... We all have friends of the opposite sex. Be careful about this; the Bible says to get your water from your own well....

14. Practice good hygiene.... I can't stress this enough---you don't like girls that smell, do you??

15. Limit the gross stuff...women don't like farting and burping as well as we do.

16. Be patient...we have been in Ephesians. Apply this one....

17. Cherish her/your children...when you provide for them, it blesses her too.

18. Choose her over your hobbies.... always choose her. She is God's gift to you.

19. Actively seek her insights...then give her preferential treatment in your decision-making process...

20. Learn to forgive...past hurts become present and future. It is easy to forgive others who fail

us on our own stuff. The Bible says to... forgive others as God in Christ forgave you. It truly is freeing to others as well.

21. Be a servant leader. All establishments have a hierarchy. It is impossible to function without one. It's not the same thing as a dictator. A servant leader example is Jesus Christ. Emulating Him is the highest goal.

22. Provide. It's more than money. It's time with her...and the bills...and time at home. Providing quality time... is just as important.

23. Dial down anger. Apply this one. Anger is a lousy motivator. The Cain and Abel legacy has haunted man ever since. No one likes an angry man.

24. Soak time. Do what it takes to have a few minutes alone together. Make this a priority. Get a sitter for the kids and stay home or do a motel or however it works for you. Make this a priority. It pays amazing dividends.

25. Verbally express your love. Speak up. Women like to know they are appreciated.

If you try and try to change and you see you cannot. Be humble and step away and don't hurt her anymore. Get help, and pray, pray, pray!

I wanted the hurting to stop. My wife and I have a new normal. In April, 2018 we were married 25 years. We are still believing for healing, but in the meantime, we are friends as each of us is healing. The time we spend together now is not perfect, but far more productive. The hurting times are few and far between. Love never fails!

Your servant,

David

Treading the Fine Line Between Hope and Reality

Often now, people will ask me how I am. It is a difficult thing to respond to because I do not have any closure. I have no clue where this will all end up, so I go day by day, and so forth. It is an amazing faith walk. So, I tell them I am treading the fine line between hope and reality. I always have the hope that God can do a miracle and heal him, but every day I am dealing with the reality of the situation.

I am dealing with singleness, but I am married. I am going to be 65, so things I did in my 20's, 30's and so forth were much easier. In some ways I am a spiritual widow. God loves widows. My husband cannot be there for me in the usual ways, but he is there, in prayer. I am there for him to help him navigate things he cannot do anymore, and advocate for him if necessary. Is it easy? No. But it is part of my call and purpose in this life. Whether he is with me physically of not, I am called to be faithful to my vows to him, and more so to this major call on my life that GOD gave me, as David's' wife. He continues to surprise me in some tender ways, and I am busy being about the other aspects of my Father's business.

Some additional struggles for myself include: deciding who I fit in better with: married folks or single folks. I struggle with sadness at the whole thing, and it is very hard to see my once viral husband dealing with his own personal limitations. My traditional identity has really been challenged, except the one that remains constant. I really have to focus on the truth that I am a daughter of the King and that will NEVER change.

Furthermore, what's amazing to me is how God provides for me those things I cannot do for myself! Too many miracles to explain. As unusual as our circumstances are, I know GOD is in them!

Just after David and I got married in 1993, he had a vision/dream. He woke up startled. He said God allowed him to see the depth and width and height of His love for both of us. He just could not get over it. He used terms like huge and enormous. He wished I could have seen the same. Yes, I wish I had. But his reaction was good enough for me and offered both of us comfort along the way.

Both of us know that we know that we know, God loves us. I could tell Dave was sincere in what he saw.

He still talks about it after all these years. That experience has carried him throughout the journey that we have traveled. We have been through so much together that I have not included in this book.

At the end of 1 Corinthians 13, God says, "*Love endures all.*" Indeed! Not only that, it says in Romans 8:28, that NOTHING can separate us from His love! God is love. God is the glue between Dave and myself. He is the glue for you, too!

I took a scriptural counseling course before we were married. Basically, this particular teacher said that in the final analysis, when our vertical walk with God is on target, He takes care of the horizontal relationships. I have seen this in action in our lives. While we think the other person needs to change, the changes God wants to make, are often in us. When we change, the dynamics of the relationship will change, one way or the other. But it started with David and me keeping God the main thing, and then sticking with it.

Every day that passes brings more healing for us both, and leads us further away from the pain. Both of us have been loosed from those strong emotions that neither of us dealt with very well. We both have soft and pliable hearts toward each other.

I can see how GOD's hand of provision is heavy upon both of us. Many miracles have happened to us, especially this year. It is comforting to know God has both of us in the palm of His hands!

Point #12: Success is not always measured in getting the result we want. It's in the overcoming.

Epilogue

How do you tie up a subject like this that has far more facets than I am able to cover here? But I, myself, have learned that hard things happen to good people. If we are able to look at the colored picture and not just the black and white version, we will see God's love and plan in it all. He does not cause evil, but he does not shield us from the hard places that will perfect us for eternity. That will make us free from those "spots and wrinkles" Ephesians 5:27 talks about, so we can stand before a Holy God. He is a bigger picture God. He will always be with us. He is looking for overcomers. He also equips us for the task!

I once wrote a blog about the fellowship of the intimacy of the sufferings of Jesus Christ. Not a terribly popular subject. However, very important. God sent His only begotten Son in a very humble way to reconcile us to Himself and provide a way to eternity. It was not an easy journey at all for Jesus. He was persecuted, mocked, rejected by His own people, sentenced to death, tortured and killed for us. He does understand what we are going through. The Bible says in Isaiah 53:3; that he is a man acquainted with grief. He is well equipped to bear our burdens, understand our feelings, and solve our problems. He has been on our journey. But He will do it His way!

He knows what is best for us.

The Bible says in Hebrews 12:2, *"fixing our eyes on Jesus, the pioneer and perfecter of faith. For the joy set before him he endured the cross, scorning its shame, and sat down at the right hand of the throne of God."* (NIV)

Jesus entered into full Sonship and the Glory of Heaven when He did this. He embraced the pain, knowing the outcome. When we embrace our pain, we enter into the same fellowship with Him. There is a fellowship of the intimacy of the sufferings of Jesus Christ that you don't hear preached very often. The natural inclination of man or woman is to flee pain. I also believe we enter into the fullness of our Sonship as Christ did, when He died and rose again. Death was defeated once and for all, and Glory was there for Him. I believe that when we do that, the Glory is there for us as well. There is always a plan. God wastes nothing. Mind you, we don't actively look for suffering, but when it is present our attitude towards it will influence the benefit we may get from it. Joseph, in the Bible, spent 13 years in prison and that was his training ground, not the palace. In one day, he was promoted!

At the end of each letter to the churches in the book of Revelation, it basically says the same thing; to he that overcomes, he will be given a particular reward. God is looking for overcomers. In all, He is there. He is in control and He will have the last word in all of our lives. Revelation 2:7

I hope I have led you to see through my journey, the other ladies' journeys, and my husband's journey to see that there is a common thread that you can cling to. Jesus is the answer. He does not always answer in our time, our way, or meet our understanding, but His ways are perfect, and there is a grand plan! His word says, He will answer us! Remember what I said, "faith makes things possible, not easy!" Hebrews says it is impossible to please God without faith. All we need to do is to surrender to Him. He will make things beautiful, even when our lives look like puzzle pieces on the ceiling. He knows what the picture will look like. Believe me, I know.

Before I married or knew David, God gave me a scripture to put on our wedding invitation. God was preparing me for my journey with David.

Indeed, the scripture was *truly prophetic!*

> *"Bless our God, O peoples!*
> *Give him a thunderous welcome!*
> *Didn't he set us on the road to life?*
> *Didn't he keep us out of the ditch?*
> *He trained us first,*
> *passed us like silver through refining fires,*
> *Brought us into hardscrabble country,*
> *pushed us to our very limit,*

> *Road-tested us inside and out,*
> *took us to hell and back;*
> *Finally he brought us*
> *to this well-watered place."*

Psalm 66:8-12 (MSG)

Other versions call it a "fat place" or "abundant place." We both are at a "new normal". I call "normal" a setting on a dryer!

However, we both are at the place of acceptance. Both of us are serving God and blooming where He has planted us. God can at any moment heal, but He tells us to move forward where we are.

This scripture was not just for us!

Appendices

Appendix A

Bible Verse References

Proverbs 3 (NIV)

Isaiah 54 (NIV)

Psalm 107

Psalm 34

Isaiah 55

Psalm 139

Psalm 91

2 Corinthians 10

Ephesians 5

1Corinthians 13

Psalm 66

Psalm 23

Genesis 37-48

2 Corinthians 4 (HCSB)

Appendix B

Points of Wisdom

Point #1: Seek the Lord in ALL things.

Point #2: When contemplating a relationship, we need to have our identity in Him established.

Point #3: God will define and establish us, not other humans.

Point #4: Expectations on other people are seldom realistic, keep your eyes on Jesus.

Point #5: When all else fails, and things look bleak, stand on the original direction and word you got from the Lord, and do not waiver.

Point #6: You will never get orange juice from a grapefruit.

Point #7: Do not yoke yourself with an unbeliever.

Point #8: God is a jealous God and He wants all of us.

Point #9: God will bring about whatever we need in our lives to develop our character. He will orchestrate situations in our lives over and over until we get it, because He loves us. He is preparing us for heaven.

Point #10: The grass IS NOT greener on the other side; it still needs to be mowed.

Point #11: Failure is part of the learning curve; it is not an end in itself. Now that is a lesson in perspective we need to keep on our 'hard drives'.

Point #12: Success is not always measured in getting the result we want. It's in the overcoming.

Point #13: Jesus not only uses 'cracked' pots. He mends them!

Appendix C

The Lord gave me a vision of how He is mending broken vessels and this is my rendition of what I saw.

Point #13: Jesus not only uses 'cracked' pots. He mends them!

"Now we have this treasure in clay jars, so that this extraordinary power may be from God and not from us."

2 Corinthians 4 (HCSB)

Appendix D

About the Author

Reverend Josephine Marie (Jo) Ayers is a wife of 25 years, a mother, grandmother, and devout lover of God. She is ordained and licensed under *Glory*

Mountain International, now *Stronger Together Ministries* since 2005 in San Marcos, California; a minister since the late 90's. More recently, Jo was ordained under her own apostolic ministry, *Flames of Fire, Inc.*

For more than four years, Josephine has been moderating a closed group Facebook Prayer page, called Esther's Intercessors, with over 100 intercessors, worldwide. Sharon Crane is now heading up this intercession ministry, under Flames of Fire.

Jo is the former Associate Director of the Greater Rochester Healing Rooms, and is also on the Mendon Fire District Auxiliary, in Mendon, NY.

Currently, Jo is on staff at New Hope Fellowship in East Bloomfield, NY, where she recently started overseeing prayer and prophetic ministries there.

Her own ministry, Flames of Fire (FOF) Ministries, Inc., a (501(c)3 non-profit corporation, was launched in October, 2016. FOF is dedicated to spreading the Revival Fire of God through His Word, individual and corporate evangelism, healing, prophecy, and worship. This ministry is based out of Macedon, New York.

Most recently she launched Prophetic Evangelism Ministry, a women's prison ministry, in hopes of developing a ministry for abused women in the very near future.

She holds women's restoration conferences and seminars called Mending Broken Pieces (See flyer in Appendix D). Contact her for more details.

The ministry mandate is to educate, motivate and activate the Body of Christ in their God given authority, with signs and wonders following. She also has a heart to raise up new leaders, especially those who have been overlooked, and have been beaten down. She has a heart for hurting and abused women.

The newest and most exciting news is the affiliation of Flames of Fire with Elim Fellowship, a national and international apostolic ministry, based in Lima, N.Y. Jo is also endorsed by her home church, New Hope Fellowship in East Bloomfield, N.Y.

She is a worshipper, author, and conference speaker. Her first book, *Prophetic Meditations on Esther – Kingdom Keys to Save our Nation, 2nd Edition*, was released in April, 2016. She is now working on a companion bible study to this book!

Contact Josephine if you would like her to come to your church or group through one of these avenues:

Web: www.flamesoffire.us
E-mail: josephine@flamesoffire.us
Twitter: #flamesoffire53
Facebook: Flames of Fire Ministries

Made in the USA
Lexington, KY
22 September 2018